Saturn
Returns

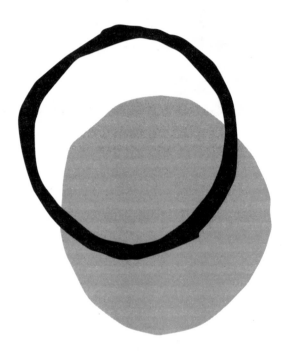

Saturn Returns

Your cosmic coming of age

CAGGIE DUNLOP

First published in Great Britain in 2023 by Orion Spring
an imprint of The Orion Publishing Group Ltd
Carmelite House, 50 Victoria Embankment
London EC4Y 0DZ

An Hachette UK Company

1 3 5 7 9 10 8 6 4 2

A CIP catalogue record for this book is
available from the British Library.

ISBN (Hardback) 978 1 3987 0419 0
ISBN (eBook) 978 1 3987 0420 6
ISBN (Audio) 978 1 3987 0421 3

Typeset by Goldust Design
Printed in Great Britain by
Clays Ltd, Elcograf, s.p.A

www.orionbooks.co.uk

To the reader, I hope this book has found you when you need it.

Contents

Introduction

I've heard it said that if your twenties are a mock exam for life, your Saturn Return is your first real assessment. When mine arrived, it seemed I hadn't been revising.

Regardless of your belief or understanding of astrology, I'm sure you'll be familiar with all the symptoms that come with this great transition that arrives in our late twenties. A sense of confusion, turmoil and wondering about your purpose in life.

For those who are new to the idea of a Saturn Return, let me introduce you. Your Saturn Return is a key astrological point in your life's calendar and is often described as a true coming of age. It takes place as the planet Saturn returns to the exact zodiac sign, degree and house it was in when you were born. This cycle takes between twenty-seven and twenty-nine and a half years, and Saturn transits each sign for a period of two and a half years. Therefore, you're likely to experience your Saturn Return between the ages of twenty-seven and thirty-one.

The years between our late twenties into our early thirties

are a key transitional time that can bring lots of thoughts and feelings to the surface, causing us to re-examine our lives thus far. When this was happening to me, I struggled to see the meaning in the madness. I now understand that this was a pivotal and important push from the Universe in my coming of age – my all-important Saturn Return.

So how do you know if you're experiencing your Saturn Return?

- You're in your late twenties.

- You're suddenly having existential thoughts about your life and the direction in which it's going.

- You've outgrown people and friends.

- You no longer have interest in the same things you did in your early twenties.

- You have a desire to change everything up.

- You feel like you're being drop-kicked in the face and every harsh life lesson is hitting you all in one go.

Since Saturn is strongly associated with structure, discipline and karma, you can bet that this cosmic event won't come quietly. In its own special way, it'll teach you all the lessons you need to live your life as the most powerful and authentic version of yourself you can possibly be, like a crash course in personal growth from the Universe. (That is until its next visit and further initiation during your second Saturn return that comes at 59. Where people tend to look back and review their lives so far, take stock and think about legacy-building.)

Confusion and doubt are likely to be a part of this process, feelings I know all too well. With this book I hope to help alleviate some of that anxiety and help you to trust that you're on the right path – to demonstrate that your Saturn Return is working for you and not against you.

This was also the key motivation I felt when launching my podcast, by the same name as this book, in March 2020. The podcast has given me the opportunity to speak to countless incredible experts, writers, spiritual thinkers and thought leaders, in turn offering an insight into some of the major themes we experience during our Saturn Return. This has provided a toolkit for how to navigate this challenging time. We've covered careers, relationships, money, vulnerability, spirituality, healing and everything in between. I've brought all of this together, along with my own experiences and insights, here in my first book, as an offering to you and to my younger self, who I know would have appreciated these teachings.

Welcome to your final initiation into adulthood. Buckle up, get ready and remember – Saturn is not out to get you, rather just to let you know this: you reap what you sow. Gulp. For twenty-seven years, I hadn't been sowing at all.

Post-Saturn Return, I can see I've changed a lot. I've grown and yet simultaneously come home to myself. I guess it's been a journey of discovery and rediscovery. I haven't figured it all out, but I'm definitely more certain of who I am and what I want. I hope that by sharing my Saturn Return journey, I can help you to gain more clarity on your own path.

I can't tell you what step to take next. My aim is simply to remind you that you already know what to do. Included are some of the practices and exercises that I've found useful, some esoteric, some pragmatic and some stories from people I've found wise. Some might resonate with you, some might not. I just want you to know that there's a plethora of knowledge and ways of doing things out there beyond the status quo. I want you to dance in your uniqueness and not be shy in doing so as I teach you how to take ownership over every part of your life. To rewrite the narrative if you're not liking the story.

The years preceding my Saturn Return were wonderful and awful, filled with heartbreaks, mistakes, different cities and different lives. They were extreme and unanchored. Sailing at full speed with no clear direction, I moved countries several times, either to reinvent myself or to find myself. Looking back, I wonder if it was sometimes just a futile attempt to outrun my own shadow. I chopped and changed careers, boyfriends, friends – and in this process, I failed, fumbled and fell. This started to feel like a rotational pattern in my life.

My early twenties were outrageous years; the brink of any new decade has the sweet scent of novelty about it. They were unusual years, in the sense that the first three were spent on a reality TV show, but in terms of the themes I'll cover in this book, these years were no different to anyone else's my age, albeit, at times, perhaps a little more heightened.

I believe your twenties are a necessary series of events, of messy experiences that provide you with the knowledge and tools you need to establish who you are in your adult life. Sometimes you only know who you are by discovering who you aren't. At thirty, after a decade of self-discovery, in a way the slate feels clean again.

We're constantly outgrowing people, places and things; our lives are always changing. This inevitable process can be daunting. But attempting to avoid change is like fighting with the tide – it'll only drag you under in the end. I hope that by sharing my story, you might feel less alone. Understanding your Saturn Return might also provide you with some tools and insight to look at life differently, as it did for me. I write as truthfully as I can about my own struggles and experiences in the process, which may resonate with some of you, but I demonstrate its uniqueness to my chart and encourage you to look into your own.

When I moved to Los Angeles at twenty-seven, something in me shifted. My behaviours and coping mechanisms that had sufficed for the last decade were wearing thin. I felt I was being shoved unwillingly into confronting a new stage of life and was being forced to look at myself head-on. And I didn't like it. The cycles I was repeating or, more accurately, the mistakes I was making were taking their toll and the repercussions felt increasingly severe. The youthful charm and naivety that I relied on wasn't working anymore – I knew better, so why wasn't I doing better? It felt like I was being shouted at by a draconian schoolteacher snapping a ruler across my knuckles – a teacher I'd soon come to know as Saturn.

A lot of the time, I felt like a disappointment. I compared myself to friends who seemed to have it all figured out. It felt as if everyone had been sent 'The Handbook of Life' and mine had got lost in the post. I embarked on this final chapter of my twenties putting so much pressure on myself – emotionally, socially, romantically – that I had the weight of the world on my shoulders, with so much to do and so little time. Time that I was running out of.

I lived these years with a 'what if?' victimhood mentality: 'What if I'd done things differently?' 'What if I'd taken another road instead?' This can be a paralysing place to be – not moving forwards, only looking back. Once you're through your Saturn Return, however, it offers you the vantage point to say, 'I'm glad things happened that way.'

As rough as it feels at the time, I believe this process of initiation during your Saturn Return is about cutting away things that aren't meant for you. It'll present you with obstacles so you can garner strength, preparing you for your next stage. It'll unburden you of things you no longer need to carry and reveal the goals you're here to pursue that are aligned with your intrinsic values. Trusting this process is the hard part.

As soon as you step out of a victimhood mentality, you start to take ownership of your life rather than feeling at its mercy. You see the role you play in everything, where you've been irresponsible and where you need to take responsibility. The societal expectation is that when you reach thirty, you should have it all figured out. At least that was the messaging I had while I was growing up.

My twenties were fun, but I'd been living for other people for so long that I hadn't really paid much attention to what I truly wanted. And living according to other people's expectations was becoming rather burdensome. It felt like I'd spent my entire life trying to be somebody else in order to fit in, chasing validation to feel loved and to be accepted but never quite reaching any point of real satisfaction. After growing tired of the charade and the people-pleasing, I decided to do something that felt almost revolutionary. I decided to be myself. But, after over a decade of pretending, I had little idea who that person actually was.

I'd lost my way, and my confidence. During those years I became very isolated. Looking back, the isolation may or may not have been necessary. It was a self-inflicted exile because I didn't know how to maintain my values and integrity and continue to develop a sense of self when around others. I didn't know how to say 'no' and would rather do what other people wanted than risk making them feel uncomfortable or disappointing them in some way. Drinking was a huge part of this and sobriety is something I cover in this book (page 189). But unlearning the belief of 'be whoever you need to be to fit in' took a lot of effort. I'd become so programmed to shapeshifting that remaining still and grounded in one version of me felt unbearable at times. I was a professional chameleon and that had been my method of survival.

In this restless unease I began dismantling the conditions I'd built over a lifetime. I began exploring aspects of myself that I'd cut away or denied, detaching the unhealthy coping mechanisms and unpacking everything that was underneath. I learned a new and very Saturnian quality: discipline. Something that was almost as foreign to me as the concept of responsibility. I departed from an old way of living – and everything that came with it – to begin establishing and cultivating my own values.

Your Saturn Return feels like coming off stabilisers: a bit wonky at first, but you eventually get the hang of it. People began to appear in my life over that time in random and unexpected ways. I was connecting to people outside of my social circle and these happened to be the people who opened my eyes to exploring the world differently, introducing me to teachers and practices I'd never heard of before. Practices that would eventually lead to me finding myself again.

When I was living in LA, I felt a significant shift and transition. I remember someone told me I was about to go through my Saturn Return, but although I'd say I was always a spiritual person, I had little understanding of astrology. I wasn't prepared for what was to come, which is exactly why I started the *Saturn Returns* podcast and why I've written this book. It was only through hindsight that I realised that was exactly what was happening. If only I knew all this then.

In a similar way that religion offers a framework and gives comfort, astrology has done that for me. Perhaps there's a construct in the chaos. A method in the madness. I've learned to take a lot more ownership over my life and become more grounded through my spiritual path. I've learned to trust in the unfolding of things, with an ever-increasing appetite and curiosity both to know and to share more. With a little help from the spirit guides I've met along the way, this book offers an honest account of my unique path, which I hope will empower people to pursue their own.

This isn't the story of someone who miraculously figured it all out. Nor is it about being the perfect you. And this isn't just for twenty-somethings – it's for anyone who's struggling to navigate the seas of change and for those who are on a quest for authenticity. I hope anyone who reads this will find solace in the knowledge that there's always hope on the other side. That I can be a friend from afar to let you know that you're not alone in what you're experiencing. Through events in my life, and the parallels of astrology, I demonstrate that it isn't all as random or chaotic as you might think. And believe me when I say it's not personal – and it's not just happening to you.

Interspersed with my stories and lessons are powerful and illuminating words of wisdom from my wonderful friend, personal spirit guide and astrologer Noura Bourni. I've gained so much from her rich and comforting insight over the years that has helped me to piece all of this together. I can't wait for you to do that, too.

**Welcome to your Saturn Return,
your cosmic coming of age.**

Part 1

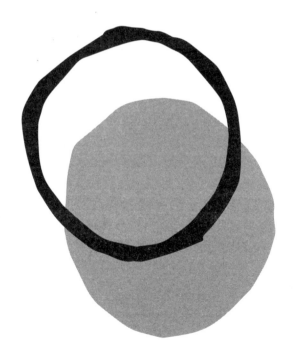

Why Astrology?

Two things fill the mind with ever new and increasing
admiration and awe, the more often and steadily we
reflect upon them: the starry heavens above me and the
moral law within me. I do not seek or conjecture either of
them as if they were veiled obscurities or extravagances
beyond the horizon of my vision; I see them
before me and connect them immediately
with the consciousness of my existence.
Emmanuel Kant

For most of my life I considered astrology a 'woo-woo' and
wacky thing, not giving it much serious thought. I associated it with vague, watered-down, generalised horoscopes
in newspaper articles that regardless of which sign you read,
all sounded applicable to you.

Being brought up within a Christian framework, I dismissed astrology, tarot and other esoteric practices that
are now part of my daily life as New Age mumbo jumbo.
Astrology was for strange people who wore baggy clothes
and smelled like vegetables. Now, perhaps I *am* one of those

strange people who smell like vegetables – who knows? Astrology's complexity, depth and rich history has only become apparent to me over the last few years and consequently, both my view and its significance in my life, as well as the general collective, has shifted.

From the Sumerians to the Babylonians to ancient Egyptians, Mayans or the Hindu civilisations, those who came before us knew the maps and codes that lay within the stars. This was in addition to the vast tapestry of knowledge within the greater cosmos around us, available for our own interpretation and guidance. World leaders and even dictators had personal astrologers by their sides, using the planet's movements to inform their strategies of attack.

Over time, Christianity and empirical science began to diminish astrology's credibility and value. After the eighteenth century, with the rise of scientific materialism, and when outer planets were discovered, astrology began its separation from science and astronomy, becoming categorised as 'superstitious', with astrologers labelled as charlatans. But it seems to be finding a renaissance within mainstream popular culture today.

For those of us for whom religion plays less of a central role, we still seem to crave something spiritual and mystical that connects us. Something beyond touch or human measure – the inexplicable, the esoteric. Perhaps because we're living in a world where we're digitally more 'connected' yet lonelier than ever, for whatever reason, astrology is seeping back into our day-to-day lives.

The cosmos and its vastness are things we may never fully understand. But they undeniably stir something within us: something we may only grasp for a fleeting moment as we stare at the night sky and realise our own insignificance within the galaxy, yet simultaneously feel how awe-inspiringly wonderful it is to be a part of it.

I believe in the power of anything that brings us out of ourselves and gives us perspective – anything that humbles us or makes us see there's something far greater at play than just our own small lives. What better way to do this than marvel at the universe around us and to indulge in the notion that there's a dialogue of sorts between these two worlds: the internal and external.

I've had many debates with friends about astrology, about the moon and its effects on us. Often, the disbelievers try to beat me down with studies and facts and counterarguments. However, what it boils down to is this: I believe that the validity of astrology and the birth chart is measured by how much it matters to someone. If it has meaning to someone, it matters. I believe that for the true expansion of our consciousness, we have to draw outside the lines of linear thought. When I look at Monet's water lilies, I don't question whether or not they are lilies, even though what I'm looking at is paint. His impression of a sunrise evokes the same emotion in me as the real thing. Astrology is for our impression and interpretation to help us navigate the collective and inner psyche. It gives us permission to feel what we're feeling and to feel seen.

Our appetite for astrology reinforces our belief that we have a destiny, and a purpose, that goes beyond the boundaries of ego. And if nothing else, it can be a great tool for self-awareness and self-mastery. It isn't fate vs free will. It's a dance between the two. Sometimes it's not in the knowing but the unknowing that paradoxically allows us to understand things and in turn ourselves. Perhaps not on a linear, logical level but on a soul one. Astrology's uniqueness is that it's both deeply personal yet simultaneously unifying. It's there for our comprehension and interpretation – both the starry skies above and the moral law within.

WHAT IS ASTROLOGY?

Before we begin, it's important to introduce you to the absolute basics of astrology and to some of the terms that I'll be using throughout this book. Astrology is a huge subject and feels limitless in what you can learn, so I encourage you to do your own research and look into what interests you. For me, I gravitated towards it as a tool for building self-awareness and a deeper understanding of self. I'm interested in the more emotional applications of astrology, and how it can affect both our thinking and our approach to life. It's a poetic means of storytelling and interpretation. Therefore, that's the focus of this book, in which I demonstrate how astrology and my life experiences run parallel to each other. In this book you'll gain a better understanding of astrology and a deeper understanding of self with a specific focus on Saturn and Saturn's Return.

Noura's astrological insight:

The word 'astrology' finds its roots in the ancient Greek word ἀστρολογία – ἄστρον (pronounced astron) means 'star' and λογία (pronounced logia) means 'the study of something or the branch of knowledge of a subject/discipline'. In essence, that's what astrology is: the study of the stars and planets and how their movements and patterns influence both mundane events and the lives of the inhabitants of Planet Earth.

From an esoteric and spiritual standpoint, it's believed that we all possess both a physical and astral body. We move through the physical realm with our physical body while still inhabiting our astral body. We move through the astral world with our astral body, freed from our physical body. When we dream and when we die, we leave our physical body behind and move through an astral world, more in tune with our eternal consciousness.

The main definition of astral is of, relating to, or coming from, the stars. It's likely to be this belief that motivated the ancients to start observing the position of celestial bodies the moment a soul incarnates, the moment we take our first breath. Over time, they've noticed that certain positions and patterns resulted in certain personality types and life events. Crucially, it revealed hints about our karma in this lifetime. In turn, this opens the gateway to living in alignment with our authentic selves, driving us to live a life that's both fulfilling and liberating.

So, what is karma? Is it a bitch? Karma is a Sanskrit word (कर्म) that essentially translates to action, work or deeds. Whichever work or action we put forth will inform the fruit of our labour. If it's moralistically bad, then you can expect to be at the receiving end of the consequences of bad karma. If it's moralistically good, then you can expect to reap good karma. However, karma unveils far more than this in astrology.

When we look at an astrological birth chart, we can see where one would be challenged to work on and improve continuously in this lifetime, for which one would ultimately be rewarded whenever it's time to reap the harvest. In traditional astrology, we can find the focus of one's life's work and life challenges by looking at different elements and combinations, including the moon as well as the north and south nodes. In astrology, the north and south nodes are a representation of our inherited gifts and our comfort zone, as depicted by the south node. By exploring the qualities the north node represents, the path we're meant to move towards using those gifts and natural talents is revealed, as depicted by its sign and house placement in the birth chart.

As any astrologist will tell you, this is a crucial part of delineating our karmic path when using astrology as a tool in pursuit of further self-development and the unveiling of one's life path. However, the primary placement that reveals essential truth, and the roots of one's karma and incarnation, is the planet Saturn and the role it plays in the birth chart.

Simply put, in astrology teachings in both the East and West, astrology stands for living out our karma and manifesting a life for our highest good. It represents the actual work (karma means work, as mentioned earlier) we're meant to carry out during our incarnation on Earth in order to fulfil the conditions of a life well-lived. With Saturn, however, we only learn what this work or karma is through pressurised life lessons and experiences that endow us with more maturity, self-containment and a broader life perspective. In turn, these Saturnian life lessons form a crucial foundation for the footprint we leave behind in this world – no matter how big or small our contribution to a healthier society. This is why all Saturn transits bring with them some type of additional burden or major life lesson so that we may enhance our abilities to withstand life's pressures while coming closer to living out our life's purpose in service of a better world.

YOUR BIRTH CHART AND HOW TO READ IT

Noura's astrological insight:

Your birth chart is a celestial snapshot or an astrologically observed moment in time from the second you were born or took your first breath. At that moment, the timer for your karma and everything that helps you to achieve your life's work was set and you were ready to go. Celestially, at that very second, the planets and constellations were arranged in a particular way, from the standpoint of Planet Earth. On the eastern horizon, a sign was rising at a specific degree. This is your rising sign, which is also referred to as the Ascendant.

From there, the birth chart is divided into twelve sections, correlating to the energies the twelve zodiac signs represent. In astrology, these twelve sections are called 'the houses'. The Ascendant marks the start of the houses, thus representing the first house. At that same moment, as the baby and the rising sign were rearing their heads, there were nine planets (seven in traditional astrology) that were transiting particular signs at a specific degree. The way that these planets are arranged from the viewpoint of your ascendant further helps to delineate the birth chart and reveal another piece of your cosmic DNA.

Like we just uncovered, there are twelve houses and

twelve zodiac signs. *Astrologically, they correlate to each other and unveil specific themes not only cosmically, but also on a mundane level – both inevitably intertwined and enmeshed in the fabric of our existence. The extent of how much this is true, especially when studying any esoteric system, seems to be never-ending, mimicking the concept that the more we know, the less we know, as each uncovered piece of knowledge leads us to want to dig deeper on our quest for truth.*

In the next few pages you'll find an outline of the key subjects and the significance of each astrological house.

The twelve zodiac signs are each ruled by a planet, as you'll see in the table below. Each of these planets, just like the houses, carries a certain energy and brings this energy wherever it's placed in the natal chart. When trying to uncover Saturn's role in our chart and therefore our life's challenges and areas of focus during our Saturn Return, we must locate Saturn's placement in the birth chart. Does it sit in the second house? The fourth house? Once we've identified this, we need to delineate it further astrologically to understand its degrees, aspects and so on, which is a whole subject in itself. However, just by understanding your natal Saturn placement, you'll be surprised by how much this reveals about the area of your life that'll require most attention during your own Saturn Return. Which brings us to the central question of this book: What is the Saturn Return?

Before we carry on, though, you'll need your birth chart

at hand in order to find where Saturn sits in your chart. There are lots of places online you can cast your own birth chart for free. Simply type 'Astrological Birth Chart' into your preferred search engine.

On page 24 you'll find an example chart of a randomly selected date of birth. This is what your birth chart would look like, except that yours will likely have different placements and sign arrangements. In this chart, if you look closely, you'll find a symbol that looks like a sickle – ♄. That's the symbol for Saturn. In this example chart, you'll find this symbol (Saturn) in the house indicated by the number nine. So, in astrology, we'd say 'Saturn sits in the ninth house'. If you look at the table below the chart, you'll find a list of planets. Look for 'Saturn'. In this case Saturn has next to it '10 Cap 29'. So, we know that Saturn was transiting the sign of Capricorn (Cap). The 10 stands for the degree it was in. So, to make the conclusion of Saturn complete, we'd say: Saturn sits in the ninth house, in the sign of Capricorn at 10 degrees.

Wherever you source your chart from, it'll end up looking something like this:

Star Sign		Dates
♈	Aries	March 21–April 19
♉	Taurus	April 20–May 20
♊	Gemini	May 21–June 20
♋	Cancer	June 21–July 22
♌	Leo	July 23–August 22
♍	Virgo	August 23–September 22
♎	Libra	September 23–October 22
♏	Scorpio	October 23–November 21
♐	Sagittarius	November 22–December 21
♑	Capricorn	December 22–January 19
♒	Aquarius	January 20–February 18
♓	Pisces	February 19–March 20

Natal Chart: Placidus
Sun Sign: Scorpio
Ascendant: Taurus

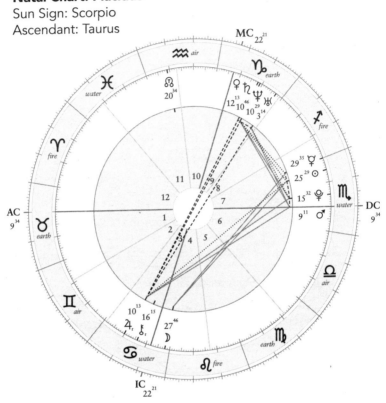

Zodiac signs

♑	Capricorn	♋	Cancer
♒	Aquarius	♌	Leo
♓	Pisces	♍	Virgo
♈	Aries	♎	Libra
♉	Taurus	♏	Scorpio
♊	Gemini	♐	Sagittarius

Aspect lines

------- Hard aspects
——— Soft aspects
.... Minor aspects

AC = Ascendant
MC = Midheaven
DC = Descendant
IC = Imum Coeli

24

	Cardinal	Fixed	Mutable
Fire			
Air		♌	
Earth	♀ ♄ ♅ ♆ MC	AC	
Water	☽ ♃ ⚷	☉ ☿ ♂ ♇	

Aspects key

☌	0°	Conjunction
⊻	30°	Semi-sextile
∠	45°	Semi-square
✳	60°	Sextile
⬠	72°	Quintile
□	90°	Square
△	120°	Trine
⊡	135°	Sesquisquare
⬠	144°	Bi-quintile
⚻	150°	Inconjunct
☍	180°	Opposition

Planets and positions

☉ Sun	25 Sco 29' 9"
☽ Moon	27 Can 46' 2"
☿ Mercury	29 Sco 34' 50"
♀ Venus	12 Cap 12' 47"
♂ Mars	9 Sco 10' 50"
♃ Jupiter	10 Can 13' 20"r
♄ Saturn	10 Cap 46' 9"
♅ Uranus	3 Cap 13' 39"
♆ Neptune	10 Cap 29' 15"
♇ Pluto	15 Sco 31' 40"
☊ True Node	20 Aqu 33' 56"
⚷ Chiron	16 Can 14' 57"r
AC: 9 Tau 33' 50"	2: 9 Gem 17' — 3: 1 Can 19'
MC: 22 Cap 20' 43"	11: 17 Aqu 0' — 12: 21 Pis 30'

Aspect grid

Body	Sun	Moon	Mercury	Venus	Mars	Jupiter	Saturn	Uranus	Neptune	Pluto	Node	Chiron	AC	Self
Sun														☉
Moon	△ -2 S													☽
Mercury	☌ 4 S	△ 2 A												☿
Venus	∠ -2 A		∠ -2 S											♀
Mars				✳ 3 S										♂
Jupiter	⊡ 0 S			☍ -2 S	△ -1 A									♃
Saturn	∠ 0 A			☌ 1 S	✳ 2 A	☍ -1 S								♄
Uranus				☌ 9 S	✳ -6 S	☍ -7 A	☌ 8 S							♅
Neptune	∠ 0 A			☌ 2 S	✳ 1 A	☍ 0 S	☌ 0 S	☌ 7 A						♆
Pluto	☌ 10 S			✳ -3 A	☌ 6 A	△ 5 S	✳ -5 A	∠ 3 S	✳ -5 S					♇
True Node	□ -5 S													☊
Chiron	△ 9 S		⊡ -2 A	☍ -4 A	△ -7 A	☌ 6 S	☍ -5 A		☍ -6 A	△ -1 A				⚷
AC				△ -3 A	☍ 0 S	✳ 1 A	△ -1 A	△ 6 S	△ -1 A	☍ -6 A				AC
MC	✳ -3 A	☍ -5 A			⬠ 1 S								☍ -6 S	MC

Your turn . . . Which house does Saturn occupy in your birth chart and in which sign? You can fill in the table below to help you retrieve your Saturn placement easily when reading the interpretations. And have a think about how your own Saturn Return might affect you from the information you see below:

Sign placement of Saturn	Notice the trouble spots as well as positive aspects
House placement of Saturn	What are my key lessons from Saturn in this lifetime?

Write out your Saturn placement here and keep it in mind as we move through the rest of the chapter:

_____

_____

_____

House	Themes and Significance	Natural Ruling Planet
First House (Ascendant)	Approach to the world – Physical Body – Overall Health – Self-Confidence – Willpower – Appearance and General Features	Mars (realm of Aries)
Second House	Values – Traditions – Speech – Wealth – Assets – Cravings – Luxury – Beauty – Comfort – Environment – Secondary Facial Features	Venus (realm of Taurus)
Third House	Skills – Hands – Community – Courage – Short-Term Travel – Relationship with Siblings – Writing and Communication	Mercury (realm of Gemini)
Fourth House	Home – Mother – Emotional Safety and Fulfilment – Private Self – Property/Real Estate	Moon (realm of Cancer)
Fifth House	Creativity – Children – Education – Hobbies – Sport – Joy – Inspiration – Development of Healthy Ego	Sun (realm of Leo)
Sixth House	Routine – Health – Healing – Mental Health – Colleagues – Litigations – Obstacles – Pets – Service – Volunteering	Mercury (realm of Virgo)

House	Themes and Significance	Natural Ruling Planet
Seventh House	Life Partner – Marriage – Clients – Travel – Business Relationships – Harmony – Fame	Venus (realm of Libra)
Eighth House	Hidden Treasures – Upheavals – Old Pains and Traumas – Sexuality – Transformation – Spirituality	Mars/Pluto (realm of Scorpio)
Ninth House	Long-Term Travel – Educational, Benevolent Authority Figures – Higher Ideals – Higher Education – Luck	Jupiter (realm of Sagittarius)
Tenth House	Status – Ambition – Stern Authority Figures – Career – Karma – Fame – Reputation – Governing Authorities – Our Projected Image into the World	Saturn (realm of Capricorn)
Eleventh House	Gifts – Bigger Community – Hopes and Wishes – Altruistic Goals – Supportive Friends – Elder Siblings	Saturn/ Uranus (realm of Aquarius)
Twelfth House	Subconscious – Divinity – Egoless Creativity – Divine Inspiration – Escapism – Addictions – Energetic Loss – Isolated Places – Forgotten Trauma and Pains	Jupiter/ Neptune (realm of Pisces)

Zodiac Signs	Ruling Planet	Natural House Association	Element	Associated Colours
Aries	Mars	First House	Fire	Red – Orange
Taurus	Venus	Second House	Earth	Shades of Pink – White – Earthy Colours
Gemini	Mercury	Third House	Air	Green – Shades of Blue
Cancer	Moon	Fourth House	Water	Pastel Blue – Sea-Green – Silver
Leo	Sun	Fifth House	Fire	Gold – Yellow – Orange
Virgo	Mercury	Sixth House	Earth	Emerald Green – Midnight Blue – Navy Blue
Libra	Venus	Seventh House	Air	Dusty Rose – Off-White
Scorpio	Mars/ Pluto	Eighth House	Water	Blood Red – Black – Nudes – Purple
Sagittarius	Jupiter	Ninth House	Fire	Orange – Yellow – Black

Capricorn	Saturn	Tenth House	Earth	Black – Blue – White
Aquarius	Saturn/ Uranus	Eleventh House	Air	Navy Blue – Violet – Grey
Pisces	Jupiter/ Neptune	Twelfth House	Water	Mauve – Pale Yellow – Peach

SATURN RETURN AND HOW IT AFFECTS US

Noura's astrological insight:

In astrology, Saturn Return represents our inner restrictions, karma, natural boundaries and, in its immature phase, is where we experience scarcity and fears. We often experience this lesser-evolved phase of Saturn when we have a prominent Saturn placement in the chart, such as having Saturn in the first, second, fourth, seventh, eighth or twelfth house, or when Saturn is influencing the Ascendant, Sun, Moon, Venus or Mars placement by aspect or sign (Capricorn/Aquarius).

It takes a major Saturn transit to help us shift out of the immature phase, which could have meant having a scarcity mentality on some level or not living authentically out of deeply rooted fears. The most common examples being a fear of failure, loss, commitment, or being alone, or a denial of one's personal beauty. So why does it take a Saturn transit to help us transcend a Saturn 'problem'? Because major Saturn transits make us face head-on all that we dread and consequently avoided. This happens so that we may realise that when our deepest fears manifest, we can empower ourselves by working towards solutions and creating healthy coping mechanisms. We learn to accept and face what scares us head-on until eventually we liberate ourselves from the shackles of an immature Saturn.

In doing so, we start the pattern of living our lives authentically by recognising our deepest fears and worries without being held hostage by them or by trying to deny them. At that stage we're bestowed with more maturity and we uncover a new-found trust in our own abilities. That's when the immature phase of Saturn ends and when the wiser, more mature version of Saturn starts to unveil itself according to its placement in our birth chart.

Saturn is also the planet of justice, duty, balanced relationships, status, humility, self-realisation and egoless service. Traditionally, it's the oldest planet in the chart and very often makes itself known in the form of delays, challenges, obstacles and uncomfortable confrontations with authority figures. It does so as a way to teach us lessons about self-realisation and standing firm in our authenticity in accordance with the themes in our natal chart.

Between the ages of twenty-nine and thirty, the planet Saturn circles back to the same zodiac sign, at the same degree that it was in at the time of birth in one's natal chart. At this time, we start to feel more challenges and obstacles rear their heads. This phenomenon in astrology is called: *The Saturn Return* – our final initiation into adulthood.

The purpose of the Saturn Return is to take stock of our lives thus far and make sure we're leading our lives in an authentic and mature way. It's shedding light and applying pressure on our deepest fears and self-limiting beliefs. It's often during this transit that we're given chances to uncover our subconsciously self-imposed restrictions and for most of us, this is the time when we start to rethink choices that we've made up until this point.

Often, we're faced with choices that might have undermined our role in society, our sense of self-worth, our relationships and, most importantly, choices that were rooted in a feeling of lack, fear and submission to societal pressures that go against our own life path. Saturn teaches us how to grow beyond our own insecurities, fears and limitations so that we may carve out a more solid, authentic and well-aligned version of ourselves as we transition into our thirties. We faithfully learn to plant new seeds for what we truly want for ourselves in our late twenties and then reap the rewards at the end of the harvest cycle in our early thirties.

So, here's how it works. Think of your birth chart as a photograph of the exact position of the planets when you were born. It's just a snapshot in time and the planets continue to orbit the sky, moving through the various zodiac signs, each being there for a set amount of time based on their pace of movement. Saturn takes twenty-nine and a half years to orbit the Earth. What this means is that after this period, Saturn circles back to the same constellation it inhabited at the time of your birth (back in your sun sign/star sign). Here, it remains until Saturn moves on into the next zodiac sign (which takes about three years). To give you some comparison, Mars takes 687 days to orbit the Earth, Venus 225 days and Jupiter twelve years.

Saturn is the second largest planet in the solar system and the sixth furthest planet in terms of distance to the sun. Saturn orbits around the sun, but because its rotational axis is tilted, this gives Saturn seasons, like Earth. However, Saturn's seasons last seven years. Saturn is ninety-five times the size of the Earth, but its density means that it would float in any ocean large enough to hold it. Perhaps indicative of the way that we should be approaching our Saturn Return is the fact that although Saturn is large, it can also be light, and this doesn't have to feel so scary.

So, when you reach the point of your Saturn Return, it means that Saturn has come back to that same position it held when you were born, back to the start. This leads to a huge moment, often viewed as a kind of rebirth, where big changes happen and we re-evaluate the way we've been living. If we're lucky, we'll experience three Saturn Returns, every thirty years – each an initiation into the next stage of adulthood. A bit like a cosmic bar mitzvah or a Holy Communion. Our Saturn Return is our cosmic coming of age.

You may start to feel Saturn's effects from the age of twenty-seven and this can continue into your early thirties, depending on your birth chart and Saturn's placement. As Saturn comes closer to its original position in your birth chart, you might feel its power more and more. In the world of astrology, this is well known as an extremely pivotal time, with its arrival bringing an assessment from the Universe, testing you on how authentically you've been living your life thus far. You may suddenly feel the pressure of time, a new sense of urgency, or have a new-found awareness of your own mortality or be faced with a somewhat sobering reality of your life (literally in my case, as I gave up drinking).

But it's not all doom and gloom, although it can feel like it at the time. Fundamentally, your Saturn Return is about showing you who you truly are. The vantage point you reach once you're out the other side makes you realise it's not happening to you, it's all happening for you. Often in our twenties we base our decisions on societal expectations, doing our best to fit in. Saturn calls us to examine our true self and use our internal resources to do so. You'll be forced to confront what you've manifested into your life, the good and the bad. If, like me, you'd been drifting through your twenties on autopilot, you might find it's a rude awakening. For some, Saturn doesn't disrupt their flow, but rather solidifies things that have been in motion for a while, as long as it's in alignment with their truth.

As a planet, Saturn is associated with discipline, structure and boundaries. If you've been living in a 'Saturnian' fashion and already embody these principles, you may simply be rewarded during this time. Marriage, perhaps, or your first child. You might secure that promotion you've been striving for or move to a city where you've always wanted to live. Seeds that have been sown might come to fruition and feel like a cementing of all you've put into practice for the last thirty years. For others, however, Saturn's Return feels like you're going through a whirlpool, turning everything in your life upside down.

Many relationships will end during this time. Promises made in youth no longer match at the core of the individual's values during this transition. Break-ups during this transit can be particularly sudden and unexpected in their ending. Saturn isn't messing around and it's going to clear your plate of anything not meant for you. As a planet, it might be slow and measured, but my goodness, you'll know when it's arrived.

Another challenge we face during this time is how to consolidate Saturn's energy into matter. Saturn is about realism – challenging us to bring our concepts and ideas into the material world. It's common during this time for people to implement an idea suddenly that they might have been thinking about for ages, like starting a business seemingly out of nowhere when it's probably been brewing in them for years. Consciously or otherwise, they're using this energy to make it their reality, and it's a great time to take those ideas and begin rooting them in the material world.

A common feeling during this time is one of frustration, because we become increasingly aware of our blocks and how we continue to get in our own way. Our conscious mind meets the subconscious, where our limitations lie. This can result in a feeling of purposelessness and an awareness of our own destructive tendencies, but it is here where we can begin to unearth the root cause of our patterns and behaviour. Having the awareness of our own polarity and owning our darkness is the best way to make friends with Saturn and use it to our advantage. It's important to remember that although it feels uniquely personal to you, we all struggle in this way. Self-awareness is the first step and if you're having these realisations, don't beat yourself up. This is where you can make real change.

Noura's astrological insight:

As we've learned earlier, we're all unique, with a distinct birth chart, and there are twelve houses in the birth chart. This means that everyone will experience their Saturn Return differently depending on its house placement and the influence it's having on other natal planets.

Below, you'll find more information on each Saturn placement. First, read the interpretation that correlates to whichever house Saturn sits in within your chart. Secondly, read the interpretation for the sign that Saturn occupies in your birth chart. Often, you'll find that both themes play a significant role before Saturn Return and are then sharply brought into focus as you approach the age of thirty.

Saturn in the first house, which shares similarities with Saturn in the sign of Aries:

The main focus during your Saturn Return will be your identity, your body and health, how you act in relation to others, your self-confidence and self-respect. Consider the following:

- How attached are you to your appearance?

- How much of it defines you?

- Are you able to express yourself physically in a way that's empowering you?

Then the Big One:

- Who are you really and who do you want to become for the next thirty years?

- How have others' expectations and views influenced your identity, and how can you show up in a more authentic representation of who you are in terms of both relation-ships and with yourself?

You might also feel a lack of energy during your Saturn Return, as if you're held back in some way, and this shows in your energy levels. It's nothing but a temporary phase, bringing the opportunity to strengthen and heal your body. It also gives you the chance to work patiently on your mundane goals while giving yourself the patience and kindness you (never knew you) deserved. You've carried burdens that weren't yours while growing up. It's time to release them and focus on yourself.

Saturn in the second house, which shares similarities with Saturn in the sign of Taurus:
The focus and challenge will be your finances, values and speaking the truth. You'll be asked to review how you treat yourself. Consider how attached you are to traditions and values that inhibit you from expressing yourself as authentically as possible. Give thought to the following:

- How does a possible scarcity mentality hold you back from stepping into a more abundant life?

- How can you start building a legacy for yourself with your own traditions and values?

- How healthy is your relationship with money – are you more of a spendthrift or can you be too frugal at times?

- What's your financial plan – can you become more financially literate?

- You may have experienced a delay in speech while growing up or have felt like your voice wasn't important. Saturn slowly encourages you to speak your truth and to feel confident in doing so, even when others don't approve.

Saturn in the third house, which shares similarities with Saturn in the sign of Gemini:

Saturn here could have brought delays in forming meaningful friendships while growing up. Even if you had a big group of friends, you might never have felt like you completely fit in. Sometimes this is a placement that can bring issues with siblings, or an unbalanced dynamic with a sibling, where one of you acts more like a parent towards the other than as a peer. This could be good or bad, depending on what extent either one of you felt burdened. This placement could also make you doubt your own skills and abilities which can make you more determined and help you to produce excellent work, or it could cause you to feel like your work will never be good enough so you give up on it prematurely.

During Saturn Return, you'll be asked to dig deep into your natural talents and skills and give them a platform on which to shine. You'll also be given the chance to heal and correct your relationships with siblings and friends. In some cases, this could make you feel like you want to change the neighbourhood in which you live. You may feel a desire to become part of a different community, where you feel able to express yourself authentically, where you can form both meaningful friendships and platonic relationships.

Saturn in the fourth house, which shares similarities with Saturn in the sign of Cancer:
While growing up, you might have felt like your emotions and feelings were a burden on those around you. If this is the case, you coped with it by suppressing them and retreating whenever you felt them arise. Perhaps one or both of your parents was/were emotionally distant or simply had burdens of their own, meaning their presence wasn't as nurturing towards you as you'd have liked.

As you near your Saturn Return, all of these feelings will likely resurface and you might find the need to open a conversation with either a therapist or whichever parent(s) you felt abandoned by. You can then use this opportunity to express each and every way you might have felt emotionally abandoned or misunderstood before. Out of all the placements, this is one that calls for deep healing and a need to bring some extra gentleness to your heart while slowly, soothingly helping yourself out of co-dependency issues that might have resulted due to that abandonment wound.

Saturn in the fifth house, which shares similarities with Saturn in the sign of Leo:
Whether you're expressing yourself creatively, or parenting, or finding joy, there's always a fear attached to it. Perhaps you don't feel that you're as creative as you are, or you have a hard time acknowledging that you

deserve joy and to be free. Sometimes this also indicates that you have a subconscious fear or avoidance attached to having children. You might love them but perhaps you don't know whether or not you'd be a good parent.

Saturn Return brings into focus your creative self-expression and it asks that you have a healthy ego attached to it. There's nothing wrong with feeling proud about a project you've just launched or a hobby you excel at or anything that you do that brings you joy. There's a need to be able to let go of fear and to allow yourself to shine without feeling guilty.

Saturn in the sixth house, which shares similarities with Saturn in the sign of Virgo:
You're meticulous, detail-oriented and perhaps even very health conscious. Not necessarily because you want to be, but rather because you've had to become so in order to feel you could have some control over your day-to-day. The majority could be driven by anxiety and burdens you've experienced due to your health or vitality while growing up.

Your Saturn Return will likely bring with it healing through confrontation of some of the fear or health issues that fuel your anxiety. At this time, you'll find that the right doctor materialises for that chronic back issue you've had for a while, for example. Or you'll read a self-help book that completely explains some of the mental health challenges you've had throughout your life. In short, Saturn Return will bring healing for you, both physically and mentally, and it'll give you the courage to let go of any self-sabotaging or self-doubt that could have contributed to it all.

Saturn in the seventh house, which shares similarities with Saturn in the sign of Libra:
You're a giver and a lover by nature, and sometimes, you might be too loving and too giving for your own good. This is a placement that could indicate a need to uncover your boundaries in relationships, both romantic and platonic. There's a side to you that can be very compromising, to the point that you make concessions with regard to yourself and your self-sovereignty in favour of some 'idea' of what you were taught love is. This is likely to sound like: 'in love, we need to make sacrifices'. During your Saturn Return, you'll be given the opportunity to review this belief system, starting with self-love.

You'll have to ensure that you have a healthy approach to your own boundaries and your own ideas of love and relationships before committing to someone long-term. You make an excellent partner, in both romance and business. Make sure that the partner you choose understands this and can meet you halfway. This will be the key to opening the door to long-lasting, loving, generous and emotionally mature relationships.

Saturn in the eighth house, which shares similarities with Saturn in the sign of Scorpio:
You might have a fascination with sex or be completely closed off to exploring that realm freely and authentically. There's no in between, which very much depicts the Scorpionic archetype. You could fear a loss of control when entering a consensual sexual relationship. On the other hand, there's nothing you want more. So, as you can tell, it's complicated. This can sometimes land you in rocky, obsessive romantic relationships or even affairs. You likely also have a true talent to explore things that are below the surface and you find solutions there where others don't. You're a natural researcher.

During your Saturn Return, you'll be challenged to review any intimacy issues you face and where they come from. It could catapult you to your very first sexual encounter or the first time you knew about sex. There will be a lot of unearthing to do, but the ultimate goal is to own your sexuality in its entirety in terms of your preferences and your innate need for total commitment and intensity once you do open yourself to having a healthy, intimate relationship.

Saturn in the ninth house, which shares similarities with Saturn in the sign of Sagittarius:
You have an amazing ability to explore different belief systems, ideologies and knowledge that help further the morality of humanity. However, there's a need for you to narrow it down to a philosophy that you can actually live by and that's authentic when it comes to your lifestyle.

There's also a theme that might play out during your life – the quest for freedom. While growing up, you might have felt stifled by teachers or father figures. During your late teens and twenties, the need to go somewhere you can feel free to express your own life philosophy authentically may have arisen, without the stern eye of an older authority figure judging your provocative stance on certain subjects.

During your Saturn Return, however, you might find yourself exactly where you were all those years ago. It's asking you to find the courage, to express your own authentic truth wherever you are – even under the gaze of those who feel most familiar and who hold tight to old belief systems that simply don't align with you anymore.

Saturn in the tenth house, which shares similarities with Saturn in the sign of Capricorn:
This placement indicates ambition and a focus on fulfilling karma this lifetime through career and status in life. A full-time mother who takes her job seriously could have this placement while acting CEO of a Fortune 500 company. The titled status doesn't matter as much as the need to be taken seriously, through their chosen duty and life path. With this placement, Saturn Return brings a completion and reward for the work that was put in, year after year. During a second Saturn Return, this could mean being able to retire and reaping the rewards of thirty plus years of diligent responsibility and work. It could also mean seeing one's children graduate and feeling a deep sense of fulfilment and achievement.

During a first Saturn Return, it could mean securing that promotion you've been working towards or seeing a project you've worked on in the background become a success. For others, it could mean becoming a parent or mentor and finding fulfilment in doing so, even though it might feel burdensome initially.

On the flip side, if one wasn't honouring their responsibilities professionally or was self-sabotaging because of self-doubt, then the first Saturn Return comes in with a rude awakening – it's time to grow up and start working both patiently and hard on your career and life goals. Because you were meant to achieve success in the avenue of your choosing and denying this would be denying your own life's karma, which Saturn doesn't take kindly to.

Saturn in the eleventh house, which shares similarities with Saturn in the sign of Aquarius:
This placement can be surprisingly positive, although while growing up, you might have felt some drawbacks. The main one would be your friendships (carrying over the theme of another socially inclined house – Saturn in the third house). It might have been harder to connect with your peers or you felt left out in some way. This could be because they actually pushed you out of the friend group in school or there was some obstacle in forming a big group of friends while remaining true to yourself. However, the friends you did have were loyal and shared a similar outlook on life – an outlook that might have seemed a bit 'out there'. But you like that. This could also cause some emotional or physical distance with an older sibling. Maybe you sometimes wished you had someone older (like a sibling) to advise you when you needed it most.

With this placement, it's often recommended that you seek out a mentor early on in your career, as you tend to be favoured by those in authority (even if you're secretly rebellious in nature). In friendships, it would be wise not to worry about belonging to or fitting in with a wide group of friends, as you tend to lose your sense of self in doing so. You find long-lasting friendships when pursuing your hopes, your wishes and your more altruistic goals.

This placement can bring unexpected gifts and income after you've taken a leap of faith towards doing work that benefits both yourself and society in some way. You have big (money-making) ideas, a big life vision for yourself and others, and an even bigger heart. The more you step into your own sense of self, the more likely Saturn rewards you materially or spiritually after it makes its return (after the ages of twenty-eight to thirty).

Saturn in the twelfth house, which shares similarities with Saturn in the sign of Pisces:
Saturn here could make you feel like you constantly have to hide your true emotions. More importantly, it might make you feel like you have to conceal your challenges when it comes to your mental well-being. While growing up, you might not always have felt supported and this in turn could have exacerbated a need to escape the environment that felt emotionally or mentally repressive. You're sensitive and creative, but this, too, is something you hide and likely have so deeply that you might even have forgotten about it.

Sometimes, this placement causes a dire need to escape through substance abuse or engaging in escape methods in other ways. It may even create fears that don't always seem rational. There's this constant need to feed into the narrative that you have to block all painful and difficult experiences because they weren't as bad as they seemed. Later, this pain resurfaces for the purpose of healing this blockage that caused this self-sabotaging behaviour.

Saturn Return could bring in a spiritual experience that connects you to your own divinity or some kind of divine inspiration that starts the process of healing. Around Saturn Return, this could also cause a need to retreat either overseas or somewhere close by yet isolated. This perhaps manifests in a minor health issue that forces you to face yourself in some way, away from the eyes of those too familiar. Creative abilities could also be significantly awakened and this in itself could work in a healing way for you. Your imagination can be vast. Your challenge is to have it work for you and not against.

MAJOR SATURN-THEMED MILESTONES AND AGES

Our Saturn Return might be the main event, but below is a list of the other key milestones from Saturn. Many people ask me whether their Saturn Return could be coming late, or early. Although that is not the case, they may well be having a visit from the great planet. As well as its predecessor, the progressed lunar return – which can be just as unsettling and happens at twenty-seven.

Saturnian Astrological Milestones	Age
Saturn Opposition We become conscious of the authority figures surrounding us and start the process of individuation. This is often a time where we start to rebel against our primary authority figures (parents, family) on a subtle level. Where we start to crave to fit in according to societal norms (media, expectations from a wider group of friends) rather than those informed by our family's views.	13–14
Second Saturn Square (first one at age seven) We feel ready to explore our own identity in the world at large. This is often a time where we start to outgrow some of the friendships that feel too familiar. It is here that we seek friendships that challenge our views or help us to grow into our own. We form more solid political opinions and commence the exploration of our values. We crave freedom in order to be able to experiment and find out what our true identity is.	20–21

Saturnian Astrological Milestones	Age
*Progressed Lunar Return (emotional preparation for Saturn Return)**	27–28
A time of finding out what's emotionally fulfilling. Relationships (both platonic and romantic) especially are brought into focus at this time. We find ourselves craving a time of simplicity where everything was informed by joy and felt less complicated. Many settle in comfortable relationships around this time because they're emotionally vulnerable. Others do the opposite and realise they no longer want the same things. They even start to entertain the idea of breaking up (often instigated right before or in the midst of Saturn Return).	
The Progressed Lunar Return emphasises our mental health and emotional well-being. It's when we look at how well we've been taking care of our inner world. Have we been suppressing our emotions and mental health needs in favour of more materialistic pursuits?	
It's a time where we often start to explore spirituality or seek help from a therapist. Here, we find ourselves craving an acknowledgement of our childhood wounds in some way. This time can feel even more emotionally taxing if we have escapist tendencies. More than any other time, it's crucial to surround oneself with supportive people and to cut out individuals and habits that drain us due to our enhanced emotional vulnerability.	
*More information in the intro of the chapter called 'Death of Self and The Fertile Void' in Part 2.	

Saturnian Astrological Milestones	Age
Saturn Return	29–30
During this time, we re-evaluate our growth so far. We look back to our first authority figures and those that came later (bosses, government) and wonder how much of their voices still haunt our personal life choices. We get ready to explore a lifestyle that might bring in more responsibilities or we finally realise that we alone have authority over our lives. This means we need to start exercising self-accountability in order to shape our lives in a way that's most authentic with our self-expression and values. Saturn Return is the most triggering yet healing of all Saturn transits if past ones weren't fully explored and repressed our authenticity. We also heal any pains and wounds that surfaced during the progressed lunar return (previous transit).	

Saturnian Astrological Milestones	Age
Third Saturn Square and the Maturation Age of Saturn in Vedic Astrology This is another crucial Saturn transit that feels more liberating than the ones before. It reminds us of our free will and gives us the courage to implement it fully. If Saturn Return acquaints us with self-sovereignty, then the Third Saturn Square completely integrates it into our being. We finally feel like a true adult and don't look outside of ourselves for any kind of authority or opinion. Controversial personal or professional choices happen around this age. Some marry the love of their lives, some leave their job and go back to school, some find the courage to move to the place of their dreams. There's a true positivity colouring this Saturn transit, even if it's accompanied with heavy choices or events. Something about it feels like we're fully stepping into our destiny. It opens the ability to achieve the most difficult love act of all – self-love. Choosing oneself over others. We're fully transcending self-imposed restrictions at this time, but free will reigns though. Some still feel like they're held back by self-limiting belief systems, which are subsequently fully confronted at the Second Saturn Opposition (below).	35–36

Saturnian Astrological Milestones	Age
Second Saturn Opposition Commonly known as the midlife crisis. Everything is brought back into question, especially if we chose suppression of our needs since the passing of Saturn Return or the Third Saturn Square. Some might feel like they've lost control (authority) over their lives. They find that so many of their hopes and wishes haven't been explored, let alone fulfilled. It can be incredibly unsettling and just as uncomfortable as the first Saturn Return due to the awareness that 'time is ticking' and we might miss out on rerouting our lives in accordance with our will. Those who took the opportunity to choose authenticity around Saturn Return and the Third Saturn Square will simply gain further authority over their lives and explore more deeply the different ideas, layers and emotions this lifetime brings.	44–45

Saturnian Astrological Milestones	Age
Second Saturn Return Here, one experiences a deep urgency to explore further what one's legacy is in this world. We want to look beyond our family unit or professional environment and move towards further lifegoals to accomplish. For some, that's preparing for retirement in order to travel the world or finally purchase that beach house we've been saving for. However, this Saturn Return also pushes a different agenda. One in which we become more selfless. We can't escape that nagging desire to ensure our voice has been heard in some way, so we might get involved in a cause we never had the time to invest in before. Or perhaps we decide to contribute to the betterment of our community or an altruistic goal in some way. Often, there's a focus on health at this time. We become more serious about check-ups and many initiate health-focused lifestyle changes around this period. Some also redefine what they expect from their friendships and relationships, even deciding to change things for the better. This Saturn transit can feel more liberating than restricting if we allow space for our intuition to guide our choices.	59–60

There's a wealth of information out there, but the table above gives you a general overview of Saturn's other key transits, which might express itself as an 'aha' moment if you're going through one of them yourself. Your Saturn Return might be the main event, but there are plenty more visits from Saturn throughout your life that are worth taking note of!

As much as we all experience similar themes during our Saturn Return, if you want a more personal insight into how it'll affect you, I encourage you to consider where Saturn is placed in your birth chart. For example, Saturn is placed in my third house in the sign of Capricorn. The third house is known as the House of Communications, which is naturally ruled by Gemini. How this manifests for me in its shadow side is that I often create polarising opinions and I can start to doubt myself. I may talk myself out of big ideas or flake when things get tough, being too perfectionistic.

My challenge is to stay on course, to communicate and to express myself when things are hard. It's to learn to handle conflict. It's no coincidence that post-Saturn Return, my career became centred around communicating and sharing information, and building an authentic community. Both professionally and personally, I experienced a deep desire to speak my truth, yet simultaneously found it difficult to do so.

For those with Saturn in the sign of Capricorn, there will be a collective theme of authority. Other characteristics that go with this are impossibly high standards. One feels more comfortable denouncing their ambition and material success, because walking away gives a sense of being in control.

Control can become both a driving and a destructive force in your life, which can become limiting. Therefore, Saturn may break your illusions of control in order for you to surrender and realise that control's underbelly is simply fear. Those with Capricorn in their chart have a strong ambition but struggle with owning this side of themselves. There's a tendency to be too hard on yourself which can lead you to talk yourself out of things that might be in your best interest.

For this very reason, I have many half-finished projects that I abandoned because I told myself they weren't good enough. I let my imposter syndrome or self-sabotaging tendencies get in the way. Ultimately a fear of striving for something and falling short. Post-Saturn Return, I've become gentler on myself and realised the selfishness in holding things in. Accountability is a big theme here; being accountable for your success and your failures can be equally scary, which before our Saturn Return we often aren't ready to do.

Fear of failure, in the way I experienced it, can be a persistent issue in your life and you can do much to protect yourself from the risks of failing – a common defence mechanism that ultimately limits you in critical ways. Fear of failure can rob you, both professionally and personally. It can manifest in an inability to commit fully for fear of the potential negative outcome, where you find yourself constantly catastrophising and procrastinating. Saturn reminds us in its way that, as the researcher Brené Brown says in her book *Rising Strong*, 'We can choose courage or we can choose comfort, but we can't have both.'

Remember that annoying teacher at school who was always pushing you to do better, picking you out from the class because essentially, they believed in you and wanted you to succeed? That real stickler for detail who, frankly, you just wanted to tell to 'piss off' most of the time. Well, that's a bit like Saturn. It's going to push you. It's going to hold up a mirror to the parts of yourself you can't see. And if you've been living out of alignment, it'll click you back into place.

Saturn can be a disruptive force in your life. Its reputation isn't commonly a good one for this very reason. Known as the 'the great malefic' or 'the grim reaper', it can cause some to become almost 'Saturnophobic' about its arrival; this isn't my intention for this book. Although I must admit, there were times when during my own Saturn Return, I wondered why this was happening to me!

I'm aware that this was down to my own victim mentality rather than Saturn's doing. Saturn builds our willpower and resilience, and there's a dance that plays out with it: if we learn to exert awareness and self-discipline, paradoxically we'll experience more freedom and more rewards.

However, if we don't use this energy ourselves to craft our lives, it'll be enforced on us.

The I Ching, an ancient Chinese divination text, tells us that 'chaos is another word for opportunity'. Things fall apart so better things can come together – and I promise you that there's a rhythm to this. So, if you're experiencing a Saturnian breakdown, I assure you that soon enough, you'll have a breakthrough.

Learning more about your Saturn Return and how it might affect you can provide you with some solace if you're going through a turbulent time, as well as some guidance in navigating the world and the cosmos around you. This demonstrates that it isn't so random, after all. Most importantly, it serves to remind you that you're not alone.

Astrology has grounded me and given me an understanding of myself. A map and language to speak that's helped me to live my life in a more meaningful way. I'm by no means an expert on the subject. I simply use it as a tool for self-awareness and personal growth, which is something I value tremendously. And if you're reading this book, I'm guessing you do, too.

We can govern our thoughts and ultimately take responsibility for ourselves. Often, what we attract into our lives is because of subconscious limiting beliefs, thoughts or inner conflict. This book is focused on helping you to understand your internal world, and how it influences your actions and experiences. Astrology is a road map and the chart truly allows for a better understanding of self. We grow through adversity, so difficult aspects, transits or placements are all opportunities to grow. It's important to know our strengths in this life, but it's just as advantageous to know our weaknesses, too. We all have an Achilles heel.

Part 2

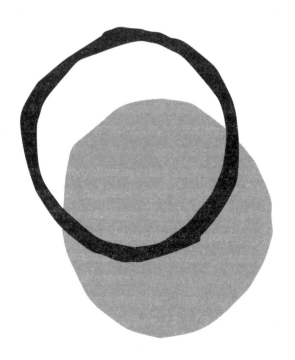

Death of Self and the Fertile Void

I have found that when I am most fully myself, and most
open about my vulnerabilities, that I have had the
greatest connections with other people.
Elizabeth Day

Noura's astrological insight:

*As we near the age of our Saturn Return, we go through
another important cycle first: the progressed lunar return.
This happens around the age of twenty-six to twenty-seven
and lasts for roughly two years. During this time, we're being
prepared to create mental space for the more concrete lessons
and opportunities for growth that Saturn's Return brings.*

*The moon in the birth chart represents our subconscious,
emotional comfort, emotional needs, childhood memories,
emotional wounds, mental state, the primary caretaker,
mother figures and our inner mother. So, when the moon*

in the progressed chart (see table: Major Saturn-themed Milestones and Ages, pages 49-55) comes back to its natal position, it triggers emotional responses to our current environment. Like a 2.5-year-old toddler who wakes from a long slumber during a road trip and finds themself far from home in a completely foreign environment, they'd need some reassurance from the primary caretaker until they adjust to the new environment. By contrast, a six-year-old would be excited to have arrived finally. They'd be more concerned with exploring and engaging in activities that bring joy and are aligned with their will.

That's what happens during the progressed lunar return, where our inner child awakens and is essentially having an emotional internal dialogue with our grown selves. They want to be reassured that they're taking care of their emotional needs and fulfilling them. It reminds us to find joy and healing, so we're given an opportunity to rediscover our true heart's desires and what gives us emotional comfort.

This doesn't mean that we allow our childhood wounds to inform our decisions. Rather, it means that we're being reminded that we're being initiated into emotional maturity. We're being nudged by our subconscious, our inner mother, to realise that we have opportunities to unearth. Not only our inner child's desires, but also our inner child's wounds. We slowly learn to differentiate between those two and try to make choices that operate out of our heart's true desires and not from a place of hurt.

Given that the moon is the planet associated with mental health, for many of us this would be the time when we're confronted for the first time with behaviours, lifestyle, and friends or partners that may have affected our mental health negatively. If up until this point, we didn't honour our emotional well-being, now we embark on a quest to a healthier, saner and more emotionally enriching way of life.

This can mean buying self-help books, making an appointment with a therapist, exploring your spirituality or simply asking for help when we need it. Conversely, when we aren't ready to face our choices and our inner child's needs for healing, it can mean indulging in unhealthy self-soothing habits and escapist behaviours. It's these that we're confronted with during Saturn's Return by way of a brutal reality check.

If we're out of alignment with what's in the best interest of our life path and well-being, the shadow phase of Saturn's Return can feel like a total identity death. Everything that we associated with ourselves and wasn't supportive of our authentic selves – the one the inner (wounded) child was hoping to grow into – starts to fall apart. We're being prepared for a complete clean slate to build a solid life foundation for when Saturn's Return fully kicks in.

This can mean having to go through a heart-crushing break-up with that person we subconsciously always knew wasn't right for us or losing a job we initially chose in service of our ego. It can also mean losing 'friends' who have *shown their true face when we set more solid boundaries as we start to shift our priorities in life. Very often, though, it means realising that everything we thought we wanted to be wasn't informed by our true will but rather by what we've internalised by societal norms. We recognise Saturn's Return when we feel the pressure and call to rebuild our identity and sense of self in service of a more authentic embodiment of our soul.*

I experienced a small amount of fame while growing up through the London-based reality show *Made in Chelsea*. The show followed me and a group of twenty-somethings living in West London as we navigated the ups and downs of early adulthood. This taste of fame was enough to give me an appetite for it. Fame is a funny thing. Unless it's the by-product of a talent, it's an empty vessel and a meaningless pursuit in and of itself. It momentarily expands the ego only to deflate it just as fast.

For a few years I thought fame was the answer. A life built and based on external validation convinced me this would give me the sense of worthiness that I lacked. We live in a world where more than ever, people aspire to be famous for fame's sake, and fame has become democratised through social media. The popularity of social media highlights our need for validation, but no number of followers or likes will give you the sense of belonging you crave. No amount of fame or money will validate you, if you don't validate yourself first.

At twenty-seven, I was still governed by these beliefs about myself and the world. I thought I had to be perfect, and that I had to be loved, liked and accepted by all. I thought I needed these things in order to belong. At that point (at an age I now know means I was going through my progressed lunar return), I decided to leave London and move to LA. Along with all the other hopeless romantics who arrive in the City of Angels, I too had big ambitions and big dreams.

During this time, I also ended a relationship with a wonderful man whom I loved and loved me deeply in return, but I'd outgrown the relationship and our paths were no longer aligned. He wanted a family and to settle down, and I craved freedom. I'd also fallen out of love with London. The city I'd called home my whole life felt tainted. Growing up in a city like London, going to nightclubs at fifteen, perhaps I'd seen too much too young. The ghost of my reality TV past lurked around too many corners in London. As did too many ex-boyfriends, for that matter.

Was I running away or finding myself? Perhaps a little of both. From the responsibility of growing up and from being in a serious relationship. From structure and reality. From life itself. I was always someone who felt happiness existed outside of me. In a person, a place. A destination point I'd never quite reach. At twenty-seven, I didn't know who I was. But I started to become increasingly aware of who I wasn't.

The internal conflict between my true nature and this creation or version of me caused all kinds of confusion. I felt an emptiness in me – one in the past I'd often try to fill with drugs, alcohol, food or love. I also felt this sense of purposelessness. These thoughts of purpose, meaning and truth, both new and abstract, circled around my mind. Moving to another country seemed like the obvious solution. Turns out, though, your shadow travels with you.

What place on Earth better represents novelty and the facade of perfection than the City of Angels? LA is a place where youth and beauty are the most valuable commodities and fame is like a religion. For that reason, it often attracts people who have an appetite for escapism.

At first, I was enamoured by LA, with its shiny coat and shiny people. You never knew what or who was waiting round the corner. The American Dream is a wonderfully intoxicating elixir in that way, drawing you in. It was overwhelming at times because I felt so unanchored as a person. The vastness of LA made me feel adrift at sea, along with all the other dreamers who gravitate there.

At this age, I often felt like I was in a tug of war between wanting to be liked and wanting to be me. My identity felt like it was based on creation, illusion, fantasy; crafted as a mask in an attempt to escape feelings of loss, rejection and abandonment. Which in turn led to a feeling that I'd abandoned myself somewhere along the way.

I started to feel this unfamiliar unease. Like every wound was resurfacing at once and my coping strategies were trying to push them back down, but they kept bubbling back up. Not that I had any idea what was going on at the time. I just felt that my life was like a sandcastle that was crumbling around me. Desperately, I tried to rebuild it, but every time the tide edged closer, taking with it another wall as it went. I was repeating the same mistakes again and again, both personally and professionally. I knew better, so why wasn't I doing better? What wasn't I learning?

These coping strategies or patterns can all come crumbling down just before and during your Saturn Return. A complete identity death so you can begin to rebuild something based on truth and authenticity. I found it hard to accept that I'd been living my life for others. To recognise I'd been driven by external validation for so long.

Saturn was about to show me that I needed to build foundations of stone. To take my time in creating a solid base. In order to do so, it would blow down my house of cards. Too many metaphors? You get the idea – shit was about to hit the fan.

In LA, I started seeing my life and the people in it more clearly. Most alarmingly, I saw myself, who I wasn't sure if I particularly liked. I'd lived like a chameleon for as long as

I could remember, creating a tapestry of characters, picking and choosing who to be for each situation I fell into. Floating around, charming everyone in sight.

As Saturn drew closer, it was disrupting my emotional landscape. I was confronted with shadow aspects of myself: my lack of discipline, responsibility and structure. My fears around my career and the direction I was going in (or wasn't going in). Unrealised expectations, my failures. Friendships that had fallen apart. The mourning of those losses with no real place to put it. I felt at sea with no vessel in sight.

The strange thing about those emotions is how unique and personal they are and feel. But what I've learned from the podcast is that many of us feel this way. Saturn's impact feels like it's breaking you open and, in my world built on make-believe, I was terrified that if I opened up, I'd fall apart and there would be nothing inside. Saturn was asking me: What are your foundations? Are you grounded at your core? Most importantly, who are you at your core? And the truth was I had no idea.

If you're beginning your Saturn Return journey, or going through your progressed lunar return, and this is something you're asking yourself, don't be alarmed. It might not feel like it, but you're right where you're supposed to be. Your Saturn Return journey is ultimately one of peeling back the layers to reveal a more authentic you.

Saturn will call on you to establish your true set of values and apply pressure where you need to grow. Understanding your chart will help to prepare you for potential pain points or tricky transits. Had I known about all this back then, I'd have asked myself the following questions:

- What do you want your life to feel like?

- What lights you up?

- What have you learned from the mistakes you've made?

- How have they helped to craft who you are today?

- What do you value most?

Take a moment now to answer a few of these questions. This exercise should stir a new perspective, and be handled with acceptance and grace. It should highlight that your mistakes and patterns all hold a purpose in defining who you're supposed to be in this world. And remember, when everything feels uncertain, anything is possible.

If I were to do this exercise now, I'd start with the following:

Q: How do I want my life to feel?
A: I want my life to feel full of magic, creativity and connection. I want to feel the freedom to keep discovering new things that light me up.

Use the following space to write your own questions and responses:

_____

_____

_____

_____

_____

_____

_____

_____

_____

_____

_____

_____

_____

_____

_____

_____

CAREER PATHS AND PURPOSE

Noura's astrological insight:

Because of Saturn's natural rulership over the tenth house of career (see page 28), it tends to bring our career path into focus during its Return. If we've been authentic in our career path and haven't let fear or internalised expectations from authority figures or society hold us back from pursuing a career most aligned and authentic to our journey, then Saturn Return brings opportunities to build on our career path. And it helps us to achieve all types of recognition and fulfilment during that period. However, if we haven't been pursuing work intentionally, in accordance with our true will, then Saturn Return can be stern (read: brutal) at its arrival.

As far as Saturn is concerned, we mustn't betray ourselves in this lifetime. Instead, we must offer ourselves a lifestyle and quality of life that's not only comfortable, but also rooted in reality with a strong foundation. It demands that you become more authoritative with yourself in fulfilling your life's work both professionally and personally, grounded in self-belief while stepping away from self-sabotaging choices.

Saturn's strong correlation with work and discipline reminds you to explore a professional occupation that's a true expression of your skills and ability, which you'll be able to build on for years, benefitting your direct environment or society at large. We're all part of a bigger picture and the work you do has to be in accordance with your authentic role within that picture. This allows harmony to exist effortlessly in our lives both individually and collectively. Even when things feel like they're falling apart, they're only doing so so that they might come together in a way that'll feel true to you, even when it's hard.

Saturn, like Earth, has seasons. Each season lasts seven years because of Saturn's distance from the sun, so it's worth reflecting on the seven-year cycle that occurs leading up to our Saturn Return. Our twenties are glamorised and sold to us as the best years of our lives and our thirties seem to be advertised as a place where everything narrows – especially for women. This pervasive fear of getting old is often felt most just before and during our Saturn Return and then eases when we're through the other side.

In our twenties, we dip our toes into adulthood but feel we have all the time in the world. We're young. We should be carefree and having fun. The halcyon days of youth and untethered ambition. Yet, on the dawn of our thirtieth birthday we're supposed to have all of life figured out.

We're expected to have found our ultimate purpose or we'll be doomed to eternal damnation. Perhaps a little dramatic, but that's how I felt, anyway.

In our early twenties, we'd say: if we aren't married by thirty, let's marry each other. As if that was an act of comradeship – to save each other from social exile and shame. Most are terrified about turning thirty. A lot even cry on their thirtieth birthday. They dread it. As if it signifies the end! But the end of what? Youth, perhaps. But bon voyage, youth. You weren't as fun as you were cracked up to be. When I turned thirty, I was pleasantly surprised to find out that 1) I didn't die, 2) life wasn't over, and 3) I wasn't socially exiled for being single and basically jobless. My thirties have been wonderful so far. I wouldn't go back to my twenties if you paid me, but for the sake of this book, let's.

As mentioned, at the start of my twenties, I starred in a reality show. This wasn't your average first job and it meant that I experienced my coming of age in the public eye, all to be consumed as public fodder and forever immortalised in the archives of the *Daily Mail*. That was how my seven-year cycle began.

I remember sitting in the dressing room at the iconic music venue The Troubadour in Earls Court. I was doing my make-up in the mirror, getting ready to perform my first ever gig while a cameraman sat behind me capturing the moment. My best friend Millie came in and sat next to me. 'Are you ready?' she asked. We were filming the first episode of a show I'd appear in as the star for two seasons before leaving abruptly. I was twenty-one years old, fresh out of The Lee Strasberg acting school in New York, where I'd lived and studied for a year.

During this time, I was going through my Saturn Square (page 50). As you'll remember, this is the transition where we feel ready to explore our own identity for the first time. Now, for a 21-year-old, this experience was a baptism of fire. As soon as the first episode aired, my world changed in its entirety. Suddenly, we were all over the press. Social media was the latest thing and there were paparazzi cameras up my skirt when I left a nightclub. The tabloids couldn't get enough. My personal life, now part of the public domain, was up for grabs and I was a willing participant. In exchange for fast fame, I'd handed it over. London as a playground had a whole new meaning. We now had an audience and people documenting our every move.

I should have been grateful, but I felt at odds. Every time someone messaged me on Twitter or approached me in the street to say something positive about the show, I'd get this knotted feeling in my stomach. It made me wonder if I'd wished for the wrong things. Historically, I've always gone for instant gratification, the quick fix. The short cut, the fast track.

At the time, my value rested on what others thought of me. External validation drove me throughout my twenties. In that world, I could continue to create this tapestry of me that I hoped would eradicate whatever truths I deemed unworthy of being seen. But after a while I began to resent this creation. I'd read about myself in a way that almost felt like an entirely different person. An entity outside of myself.

My disdain for this version grew. Ostensibly, I was doing well. I was making a bit of money, I was a little 'famous' for fame's sake, and I was going to lots of parties and having a lot of fun. But this version of myself was getting out of control. Like the Hyde to my Jekyll. I was on a one-way self-destruct mission. My behaviour became more reckless. I started missing jobs, not showing up for things. Generally being incredibly irresponsible. This was largely because of my partying. But that was a symptom of something deeper.

As these two versions of me became more polarised, I leaned further into my sabotaging ways. As the version of myself that I'd created was out-shadowing my true self, I feared I may dissolve entirely if I continued down this path. For the majority of my life I'd so desperately wanted to disappear and now, through fame, I was. My behaviour was so normalised within my circles that it was hard to know something was wrong. I could see the train I was on, the direction it was heading in. And I could see the possibility of addiction if I stayed on this track.

Then, at age twenty-three, I went to Australia with fellow castmate Oliver Proudlock over the Christmas break, having wrapped the second season of *Made in Chelsea*. The show was growing, as was my exposure, and everything felt out of control.

While away, I decided to quit the show just as it was reaching its height. I emailed the head producer explaining my decision to leave. I was expecting World War Three to erupt, and rightfully so. She'd made me the star of the show and it felt like I was being unappreciative by leaving. But she calmly replied that she understood and asked to meet when I returned to London.

On my return, I remember taking the tube to NBC's offices. Both the producer and the head of the network were there. He was over from LA and wanted to discuss my decision to leave. After pretending to be calm and in control, I realised that actually, this was a mission meeting for me to stay. He was dressed in an expensive suit, well manicured and charming. Even though I didn't know him, he knew all about me. He started telling me about things we could do in the show for my storyline, about the doors he could open in LA. It sounded exciting, but at this point, my mind was made up.

'Is it about the money? Because if it is . . .' he started.

To which my producer interrupted. 'It's not about money.' She knew me well at this point and she was right.

'So, what is it you want?' he said challengingly.

I thought about this for a moment before replying. 'Normality.'

He smiled at me with a knowing smile and said, 'Honey, trust me. It's overrated.'

A big Saturnian lesson for me has been that the karmic bank of the Universe doesn't miss a penny. It all comes full circle one way or another.

I'll never forget that line. You know, he might have had a point! But at the time, I felt like a hot-air balloon taking off without a rope or any means of coming back down. I didn't feel like the master of my fate – merely a bystander, sitting uncomfortably in the passenger seat, unsure of where I was being taken. And for all the fame or monetary success I may have experienced had I stayed, I don't think my soul would have been OK.

If something isn't rooted, it won't weather the storm. You know what they say: what comes easy won't last and what lasts won't come easy. Saturn, by contrast, is all about focus, diligence and the long game. I find it a beautiful irony that someone so un-Saturnian by nature is writing a book on its very themes, but that's Saturn for you. Where we meet and overcome our adversities is when we create something worthwhile. Saturn isn't here to make you struggle. It's here to turn your struggles into strength. This is why Saturn's lessons have been my most valuable ones, because they've felt so foreign.

The two years I spent on the show were a whirlwind.

Filled with manic highs and many dramatic lows. I lived those years wildly, without much thought, consideration or care – either for myself or perhaps sometimes those around me. The day I quit was a pivotal moment and I still respect myself for making that decision to leave. I also realise my immense privilege in having had that opportunity in the first place. Many would have loved to be in the position I was. But this book is about a journey to authenticity and that requires making decisions not everyone from the outside is going to understand.

Looking back with, *hopefully*, more wisdom now, I'd have advised myself slightly differently. It's this advice that I'll share with you now. If you want to make a bold decision, fantastic. But have a plan. When she came on the *Saturn Returns* podcast, Lacy Phillips, a leading manifestation advisor, described it as having a 'f**k you fund'. This means when you go to make that bold decision to quit your job (which is essentially what I did) or embark on something new, you must have three months' income to support you that allows you to go out alone and follow your dreams. And if you're going to say a metaphorical 'f**k you' to the head of a network and walk out of a hit TV show, you'd better have a bloody plan.

I didn't. I had no agent, no management. No real plan, but when I got back on the tube to go home, I was so sure I'd made the right decision because I could feel it in my bones. But I was unsure what to do next.

Without a plan, you risk meandering through the void. A plan, however, gives you a pathway through. So off I went, meandering through. Throughout the next seven years, I went on a long journey of self-discovery. Exploring various careers, I launched the clothing brand ISWAI, wrote a dating column for the *Evening Standard*, wrote and performed music, engaged in auditioning, and moved to Australia and then LA. I felt close to things but things struggled to connect. Like something was holding me back. And as time went on, I felt like I was being left behind by the herd. It felt like everyone was forming their lives into some sort of meaning and structure and I was shackled by the past, by my own fears and perceived limitations.

When I arrived back in London in my late twenties, all I felt was lost. I didn't know it then, but within that lostness was an opportunity to be *truly* found. And there's no better guide to bring you home than Saturn.

Saturn's shadow side can manifest in fear. Many of my decisions have been on gut instinct and intuition, especially when I was younger, but as I've got older, fear has stepped in and sabotaged things. This is still something I have to practise balancing, knowing my fear holds a purpose to protect me, but it also gets in my way. When we're walking a path that others can't see, or they question, fear wants us to turn back, for it also questions the unknown, the unfamiliar. It makes false stories out of it.

On the road to our authenticity, fear is the antithesis of the faith we need.

Perhaps that's why your Saturn Return comes at just the right time, during your twenties, after you gather these experiences. It sets you up with the knowledge to be the master of your fate, because to be in the driver's seat you'll have to rub up against the edges of the status quo. Often, to build your own sense of authority and to realise your worth, you must experience the powerlessness and struggles that come before. This will come with age, and often post-Saturn Return, which is why people suddenly knuckle down and start believing in themselves at that very point.

Having the belief of others is wonderful, but trust me – it's not enough if you don't believe in yourself. I've had many opportunities throughout my life. I acknowledge that I was dealt a good hand, but what I lacked was self-belief to utilise those opportunities. Fortunately, the draconian lessons of Saturn allowed me to craft self-discipline, self-belief and self-love. Through these principles, I'm able to lead a life that's fulfilling and authentic.

DEATH OF SELF AND THE FERTILE VOID

CHANGE AND LETTING GO

Noura's astrological insight:

A common stage during Saturn Return or a Saturn transit is a sense of relief. Like we've arrived. We can breathe and relax; we feel like we're past the worst. We've seen the lessons, we've heard the lessons, we know the lessons and now we're desperate to move on from them. As the dust starts to settle and life seems deceptively calm, we encounter the next stage of Saturn Return, which is the implementation of the lessons. It gets us to look at the following questions:

- *How are old limiting beliefs and approaches to our lives still influencing us?*

- *How ready are we for the next chapter of our lives?*

- *Have we passed the test?*

- *How much do we still care about society's gaze upon our personal choices that fuel our growth and honour our joy?*

Well, at this stage we're bound to find out. This is a stage that can feel just as jarring as the initial stages simply because we underestimated how ingrained some of our behaviour and certain expectations were. We didn't appreciate how hard it is to remain authentic to our path at all times.

As we navigate this stage, which could be in the form of an obstacle at work, at home or in pursuit of a goal we set for ourselves, we learn the necessity of surrender and the virtue of listening to the guiding voice that is our intuition. We further develop this virtue in ourselves and slowly let go of the past as we embrace the present, while surmounting the obstacle or experience that triggered it all.

I believe a key component to navigating the turbulent waters of life, relationships and Saturn's Return is changing our relationship to change. It's one of life's certainties, after all. And although things may feel like they aren't going your way, I believe life is always redirecting you to something better. It's just making sure you pick up a couple of lessons along the way, packing your bags with the wisdom you need.

In order to switch this mindset around change, we must learn to go more willingly with the tide rather than resist it. Through change, good and bad, we grow. I like the analogy that we come into this world like clay, unformed and unbounded. The pain and experiences we go through are a necessary process in order to become something beautiful. Like the pressure of the hand that sculpts the clay, this is the process of our becoming. This is our Saturn Return; we can't stop it. So, we might as well alter our relationship to it.

It's my personal belief that astrology can really help with this. Having a basic understanding of your chart can help to alleviate feelings of guilt, shame or regret. It gives an overview of your life, a bit like a satnav that shows roadworks. Or the weather forecast showing a storm. Except astrology gives it meaning.

If we can relinquish control yet take radical responsibility for ourselves and our lives, that's where freedom lies. Authority and personal sovereignty are often foreign concepts to most of us before our Saturn Return. Some even use astrology as an excuse, a cop-out. But astrology doesn't negate free will. We always have choices, and there are multiple avenues you can go down. Things aren't fixed or rigid – they're mercurial.

Mercury being in retrograde doesn't mean everything is going to go wrong and you have no power over your life at this time. Nor, for that matter, does going through your Saturn Return mean everything will crumble around you and that you're merely a bystander. Astrology gives you a map of your life, highlighting pressure points and tricky transits. It's to be used in harmony with our own internal navigating system, trusting our intuition, our gut. We have to be able to discern things for ourselves while using these esoteric tools to deepen our inner knowing.

THINGS FALL APART (SO BETTER THINGS CAN COME TOGETHER)

If I could give my 23-year-old self one piece of advice, it would be this: the only wrong step is not taking one. Don't be scared of fucking up and letting things fall apart. In our twenties, we put far too much pressure on ourselves to have it all figured out when really, we're still uncovering and discovering ourselves. We need these messy experiences in order to do so. We need contrast. We need to know what feels off to know what feels right and in alignment.

In a world that seems almost immune to pain, we don't know how to acknowledge the signs within our own discomfort. The nudges along the way. We disconnect from our intuition by drowning it out with noise. In your late twenties, you'll feel caught between a rock and a hard place. They're undoubtedly some of the most challenging years of your life when it comes to happiness and knowing yourself.

Listening to your peers, your family and society might feel in conflict with listening to yourself. This tension is good, although it might not feel that way. Much like the mystical process of an oyster creating a pearl, Saturn is like the grain of sand in the oyster, rubbing up against you, forcing you through your challenges. Not in spite of them, but to evolve into something more refined and more beautiful. You may not feel this day to day, but in the long term, your Saturn Return is a pearl in the making.

As Saturn breaks things down, it does so to build you up. During my early twenties, I'd parted ways with a version of myself that didn't feel authentically aligned with me, but I continued to seek my identity outside of myself. On one hand, I hated being told what to do, who to be. But at that time, I didn't have the courage to be confident in what I wanted for myself. I continued to be told who I was in the world.

During my time in LA, I was focused on music, but within that industry was a whole load of people spinning me in different directions. Telling me I was too old to do pop music, too posh to be relatable. Work with this person. Change your name, your style, your sound. Everyone had a different opinion, yet not one person told me it was OK to be me. I felt dizzy with all the conflicting advice and all the noise. Internally, something was stirring.

As Saturn moves closer, we often begin to feel this intense pressure of time and a feeling of frustration. The awareness that it's a limited source that we might be running out of and the fear that our window of opportunity might be closing. Saturn implores us to look at the clock. Its glyph is the sickle of Chronos who's the god of time. If we're out of alignment with what's right for us, the awareness of time can be one of Saturn's most brutal lessons.

I'd let my entire identity and self-worth become so dependent on the success or failure of my music that if it failed, I was a failure. Anxiety began to build in me, time felt like it was slipping away, the window of opportunity felt like it was closing before my very eyes – and I stood in front of it, motionless and frozen.

One day, when I was driving to the studio in Burbank, California, this pressure cooker exploded, which was when I had my first panic attack. This was brought on by a culmination of factors: being away from home and family, being unsure of my life professionally and the direction in which it was going. Resulting in a deluge of emotion. I was crying so hard I couldn't breathe and I had to pull the car over. My mum had to calm me over the phone. I was trying so hard to control everything, but the more I did, the more out of control everything felt. Life felt so unsure and I felt powerless. Like I was waiting at the gates to my fate and no one was letting me in.

We often measure the time we've invested in something as the sole reason to persevere. That's not to say it's invalid, but Saturn can make us feel truly at odds about this. A relationship that lasts for several years doesn't make it a success just because it's lasted a long time. Nor does it become a failure by its ending. Same goes for the pursuit of a job or career. We struggle with allowing ourselves the freedom to change course. This is an illusion that Saturn pulls the curtain on. But the more I continued to look outside for the answers, the more resistance I faced. The harder I searched, the more lost I felt. Saturn was urging me to look within.

Shortly after, I decided to return to London and re-evaluate things. I needed to be home with my family and familiar friends. During this time, I felt a lot of shame. It seemed each time I was close to finishing something, I'd abandon it at the last minute. The closer I got to releasing music, the more anxiety would come, convincing me I didn't want it, self-sabotaging in all kinds of creative ways. I didn't know it then, but I was being entirely driven by fear. Fear of failure, not being perfect and of being judged and ridiculed. I didn't know what else to do but retreat home. Looking back, I think this was my rock bottom. And in hindsight, perhaps that was the beginning of it all.

ROCK BOTTOMS AND SPIRITUAL AWAKENINGS

Noura's astrological insight:

Saturn can certainly delay or cause the ending of certain situations, relationships and plans that we envisioned for ourselves. It does this only until we achieve the maturity to take the next step. Otherwise, it brings about the ending of things because whatever we thought we wanted, wasn't for our highest good. It sounds like an old wives' tale, but Saturn is old, so I'll say it: 'Everything comes in due time – what is for you will not miss you.'

Which brings us to another theme that the onset of Saturn Return can highlight – the art of letting go. When you're able to let go, you're able to create space for truth and so behind this quest for universal truth is the motivation to personalise it somehow to our own life, our own approach. We're led to the past, where we clearly start to uncover patterns that paved the way towards the emotional rock bottom we all experience at some point during the Saturn Return, no matter how brief.

The truth that we uncover during this dark night of the soul is all that we need in order to recognise what sparks authentic joy in us. Which is what Saturn was nudging us towards all along, even if it came with destruction first. The fertile ground it left behind allows us to plant seeds and cultivate a garden of our own, where we'll have found the space to connect with creation and the divinity behind it all. In turn, this causes both spiritual evolution and also a more mature, sober and realistic outlook on the cycles and seasons of life.

Coming home to London was a strange experience, as anyone who's travelled and lived abroad will tell you. You feel like everything has stayed the same, but you've changed in every way. I'd created this body of work while in LA with help from the amazing people I met, but now was the time to put it into the world. I'd cultivated discipline, but on its shadow side, its inverse, perfectionism had taken over. Perfectionism has pulled me away from much joy. The underbelly of perfectionism is the fear of not being enough. I gripped so tightly to my music that it was almost impossible to release. I came up with every excuse under the sun. Excuses I eventually ran out of.

I decided to release a song independently in the summer of 2018, called 'Here We Are Again'. The song was a story about when I met up with my ex-boyfriend by the River Thames outside a pub in Putney when I was twenty-seven. I'd written the song with two friends of mine in Venice Beach. I put together the visuals, made a video with DIY videography and released it on 4 July 2018. I was on holiday with my brother at the time, on a road trip through Italy. I remember sitting in the kitchen of an *agriturismo* (farmhouse) in the hills of Tuscany, trying desperately to get Wi-Fi so I could check whether anyone had listened to the song. (Not exactly the dream execution for a music release.) We went for a walk that afternoon and I felt panicked. Releasing music felt so vulnerable and exposing.

'What do you need to do? What do you want to happen?' my brother asked.

'I want to get on New Music Friday,' I said.

'How do you do that?' he replied.

'I have absolutely no idea.'

A few hours later, I was back in my room getting changed, when a WhatsApp message appeared on my phone. It was someone from the music industry who I hadn't spoken to in years. 'Congrats on New Music Friday!' it said. What?! I opened Spotify and there it was: 'Here We Are Again'. Not only in New Music Friday in both the UK and USA, but all over the world!

The song suddenly started picking up streams – 100K, 200K, 300K. I was getting messages from fans telling me how much they liked the music, what it meant to them. It was honestly one of the best days of my life and I burst into tears. I couldn't believe it. Why had I held back and held on for so long? I'd denied myself something I loved for years because of my own fears and self-doubt.

Even though this moment was a real victory and a step forwards in my journey of self-belief, I couldn't shake this pervasive feeling that I was still seeking approval from others. I still didn't feel I was enough.

Shortly after turning thirty I went through a break-up that knocked me. In the midst of the heartbreak, I decided to go and see a healer that my friend Farleigh recommended. Even though I had some good moments with music, I felt off course in life. The one thing that I felt was stable – my relationship – had disintegrated before my eyes. The break-up ignited all the other uncertainties in my life that I was denying. I felt like I was on the wrong track, no pun intended. but I also felt too far gone to turn back. I took my mum's car and drove down to Henley one afternoon in late September – a beautiful place where I'd spent a lot of time as a teenager.

Valesca the healer greeted me in the back of a picturesque little garden. She was younger than I expected and quite beautiful. She took me into a hut built at the back of the garden away from the main house; it was small and quaint. She welcomed me inside with a warm and inviting energy. I lay on a small bed and she stood by my feet, seemingly reading the energy emitting from them. As she did, Valesca started asking me questions about my life and what I did. I told her I was a singer.

'Hmm. It's not resonating in your body,' she responded.

Slightly disheartened by the comment but not entirely surprised, I replied sadly, 'I know.'

'Keep going,' she said. 'Tell me the thing you love to do.'

And so I listed all the things I loved to do, as well as singing. I talked to her about poetry, how I loved the art of storytelling, truth-seeking, performing, connecting with people, acting, writing, astrology, spirituality and holding space.

She smiled at me and nodded. 'These are all true,' she

said, 'and these are all things you must do.'

Now I was thirty, I thought I couldn't possibly change direction. Plus, it seemed like a long list. And which one of these was I to pick as my career? I'd always been told you have to focus on one thing to be successful at it. But after our session, she gave me some advice that I've never forgotten. She told me that I needed to open up my language around what I did, because I was being closed off. I was so fixated on one particular path that I was missing opportunities. She told me that all the things I wanted to do were possible and would lead to a career. Because they were true for me, and I shouldn't be ashamed in saying so.

If hearing Valesca's advice hits you the way it did me, take a moment here to consider all the things you'd love to do and have yet to try. These may or may not be pursuits you want to make a career out of, but they might bring a whole lot of joy into your life.

To get you started, if I were to write it down, it might look something like this:

I love singing and songwriting and want to be better at playing the guitar so I can write songs more easily. When I'm immersed in creativity, the concept of time vanishes, and so does the outside world. Poetry allows me to alchemise my feelings and emotions and offers a snapshot of a moment in time. One that years later I'll read and remember exactly how I felt and what was going on.

Use this space to list activities you enjoy here:

_____

_____

_____

_____

_____

_____

_____

_____

_____

_____

_____

_____

_____

_____

_____

_____

I'd been conditioned to think I needed to be just one thing. That I had to try to fit into one box. I believed that there was a particular trajectory I had to go down, no matter how much resistance I faced. I'd lost sight of my 'why' and realised I was still living for other people's expectations and validation. I felt like I'd committed to something for so long that I had no choice but to continue to pursue it. I was afraid of what it meant to change course at thirty. To admit that I didn't have it all figured out. I attached so much of my worth to what I had or hadn't achieved that Valesca encouraged me simply to let go. To let go of the outcome and focus on what was true for me. To place my attention on what felt aligned and authentic. And to let go of the pressure and the shame.

I decided from that moment to focus on myself, and around three months later, I moved past the break-up and the anxiety about my future, and I've never looked back. In fact, I'm so grateful that the relationship fell apart. It broke me open, but in that void, everything I have now grew. Everything Valesca said about my career was spot on. That meeting allowed me to take off the backpack of opinions and expectations I'd been carrying uphill along a winding and uninviting mountain path for most of my twenties and change direction. I started running downhill again, not entirely sure where I was going. But for the first time in a long time, I didn't care. I felt free.

The shift was this: I became more curious about my purpose, seeking it from an intrinsic place, rather than in the pursuit of accolades. I started a quest for authenticity rather than focusing on the facade of success. And perhaps most crucially, I let go of the idea that there was a path I should have chosen differently, the road I never took. I relinquished my goal or fantasy of having a different past and finally embraced the unknown. Looking back at my chart, this was right when my Saturn Return ended, in October 2019.

SPIRIT GUIDES

When we hit our rock bottom, we often find the sort of spiritual guides and teachers who offer us these really formative moments in our lives. I view it like this: when the path is darkest, people will provide you with a lantern in the strangest and most unexpected of ways. They'll often seem totally random. Pay attention to those people, and the signs. They aren't coincidences. They're your guides! Whether it be a chance encounter with a stranger that you never forget or the reappearance of an old, good friend, list some of yours here. Think of all the synchronistic moments in challenging times when people have appeared almost out of nowhere, and how that's informed and guided your path, nudging you further towards your truth.

Through trial and error, towards our late twenties we begin to have a better idea of who we are in the world and what we want for our future. Forging our own reality, with a new and more developed sense of self. This isn't without its difficulties. Since Saturn is a major indicator of one's career, your Saturn Return often changes or coalesces your path, often quite abruptly. During this time, you'll notice many people will quit their job to follow their true passion. Starting up a business from scratch or dramatically changing course. It's at this time that we get that sense of 'it's now or never'.

A trickier aspect is when we've started something and it just isn't working. We know it, our friends know it, the bank balance knows it, but changing course seems too daunting. There's a very fine line between sticking at something you're passionate about that has the potential for development and continuing to drive down a dead-end street. Only you know and feel the difference (or Saturn might be nudging you). And being truthful with ourselves, and having the courage to change course when necessary, is nothing to be ashamed of. In fact, it's a strength. Good things take time, and you have time to figure it out. Life isn't about not making mistakes. It's about how you handle them and what you learn from them when you do.

American journalist Mary Schmich wrote a piece in the *Chicago Tribune* in 1997 titled 'Advice, like youth, probably just wasted on the young.' It's one of my favourite pieces of writing, so wise yet so simple. One of my favourite lines is 'Sometimes you're ahead, sometimes you're behind. The race is long and, in the end, it's only with yourself.' So, she implores the listener not to feel guilty if they don't know what they're doing with their life. Don't worry about not having a clear direction right now. Don't compare yourself to your peers. Trust the timing of your life and stay in your own lane. You can find your purpose at any time, and it doesn't make you any less brilliant if you haven't found it yet.

Regardless of your interest or belief in astrology, the pressure we all feel approaching thirty is undeniable. But the truth is the majority of this pressure is the result of internalised societal expectations and cultural dynamics at play that have conditioned us to feel a certain way about ourselves and lives. It's not rooted in reality. We get to choose what we decide for ourselves and how we want our lives to be – they are ours, after all. So, throw out the rule book, question what beliefs are yours versus what you've been told to believe and enjoy the freedom that is the blank canvas of your life.

Saturn often arrives as a fork in the road when it comes to discovering our purpose. If we've been working hard and are on the right track, this can simply mean levelling-up. If you're uncertain of where you are or what you're doing with your life, Saturn will bring it to your awareness. You may have known this was something you're struggling with, but Saturn won't let it slip by. The theme will reoccur in your life until you become conscious of it. The obstacles will keep coming up until the lesson is learned.

This can manifest in a 'rock bottom'. Although not commonly viewed as a good thing, I think rock bottoms and spiritual awakenings run synonymously with each other. Once we've slammed ourselves against the wall that doesn't yield for the final time and our ego has no more answers, the ego views this as a tragedy. But this is an opportunity for transformation and growth. A spiritual awakening requires an ego death. We must dare enough to reimagine a new vision for ourselves. We must accept the death of ego and all things inauthentic.

Saturn helps you to identify your life lessons and overcome them. Once you've found where your challenges are, don't fret. If you have hit a rock bottom, its actually an exciting moment! Although it's uncomfortable and feels icky, you should celebrate. This means you're ready to begin your journey of self-mastery. This is an endless but nourishing quest. Saturn rules success and excellence, and its lessons are all about refining and becoming the best version of yourself.

When we work with Saturn, we'll quickly reach that 'aha' moment. A moment of clarity where everything you've learned begins to crystallise. A time when you realise that if you want to be successful and achieve your dreams, you'll have to commit to overcoming certain obstacles.

No one said it would be easy. Saturn isn't about shortcuts, it's about diligence and hard work. For those of you sighing at those words, trust me – I get it. I've tried every shortcut in the book. This period of life is all about rooting things in reality and that demands your full commitment. It requires meeting your problems and shadow aspects head-on, dealing with them and continuing forth. The trial, the test, the triumph. The breakdown, then the breakthrough.

Your Saturn Return is the perfect opportunity to make really positive changes in your life. If you learn to work with the forceful energy of Saturn, it'll take you out of situations no longer serving you, such as dead-end jobs, and away from deadbeat friends. Simply surrender to it. Trust that the Universe is guiding you. I invite you now to consider these questions:

- Are you in flow?

- Are things naturally aligning with ease?

- Does it feel light?

- Or does it feel heavy?

More often than not, it's our resistance to things that causes us the most pain, and our inability to relinquish control.

I believe these moments of rock bottoms and spiritual awakenings crystallise and develop our strategies for life. They force us to change course. It's a great misconception that people just wake up and know who they are. It's within our lostness, our isolation that we're forced to discover ourselves.

WHAT BRINGS YOU JOY?

Although music isn't the main thing that I'm doing anymore, I think it's important to note that nothing that brings you joy is ever a waste of time. Nothing you learned from is worth regretting. No relationship is a failure simply because it ended. I spent a lot of time in my twenties living in a paralysing state of regret, but during my Saturn Return, and through the lens of astrology, I've realised all those trouble spots, or seemingly dead ends, were necessary detours. For which now, retrospectively, I can be grateful.

Into our thirties, as pressure increases, we readily disengage from our creativity if it's not how we make a living. We stop playing or learning if it's not our 'job' or an earner. You often see during people's Second Saturn Return (approaching sixty) that people start to take up things like the guitar, the piano, singing or painting. Through experience, they've realised the importance of the simple pleasures of life, in the pursuit of joy, in their next initiation with Saturn.

Creativity not only brings us inner peace, but it also allows us to continue to be playful. It's good for the soul. Pursuing my creativity during my twenties allowed me to become more grounded, more self-aware. More considerate. My life and career have pivoted, many times. Which I'm sure they'll continue to do. I could never have predicted how it would have unfolded; I'd never have imagined I'd be writing a book or working in the spirituality space. Or doing all the amazing things I get to do, speaking to some of the greatest thought leaders out there.

But that's the beauty of it. I no longer regret anything like I did during my twenties, because it all led me to where I am now. But I do wish I'd been a little less hard on myself. I'll continue with music not because I want to break into the industry or become a pop star, but because it brings me joy. It's a form of self-expression and self-discipline, which I see as another spiritual practice.

I believe we'd all be a lot happier if we nurtured our creativity and hobbies a little more. Made more space for the things that bring us joy, not just money. For when we're doing these things that light us up, we're our most magnetic. I try to apply these principles to all aspects of my life. To focus on the details a little more, to commit to what I do more fully. I've come to realise that these are our foundations – dedication, discipline and commitment – and the bricks that you build a home with in order to create a life of meaning.

By this I mean dedication to life holistically and to loving yourself and showing up for yourself. It's the building of little details – the daily practices and rituals and those little wins – that over time amount to something meaningful. Something happens energetically when you do this, so it's important not to worry too much about the 'How do I know it'll work?' too much (because that usually stops us from starting). It's the laws of attraction. When you send that energy out into the Universe, it'll deliver. Saturn is all about rewarding hard work. Applying yourself will give you the necessary tools, so don't be afraid about it not working out. It might not be meant for you. But it'll prepare you for whatever is.

DISCIPLINE VS PERFECTIONISM

Noura's astrological insight:

There's this notion that Saturn is associated with constant work in the pursuit of perfection, which is rooted in the fear of failure. Just like everything else, Saturn has its positive and negative expressions. The negative expression is apparent when one's early life (before twelve) was riddled with a sense of insecurity or scarcity or excessive criticism. In these cases, Saturn acts up, as an attempt to protect us, increasing this fear of whatever it is that makes us feel 'less than' while growing up.

It does this so that we tell ourselves that we never want to feel that way again and as soon as we gain some indepen-

dence or have an outlet to express our abilities, we try to overcompensate by overachieving. Doesn't sound that bad, right? It isn't. So long as this need to overachieve isn't rooted and motivated by fear. Which often it is. Fear of lack, criticism, attack on self and so forth. So, as we mature and we near our Saturn Return, this constant need to be perfect or to appear perfect in whichever area of life is most relevant to us begins to turn into a type of anxiety or self-sabotaging behaviour that can start to rule our lives and push us to seek help or advice.

This is the first step where we start to feel a more positive expression of Saturn. The side of Saturn that at its Return gives us the tools to re-parent and re-educate ourselves, and to prioritise our mental well-being. It's only when we're able to transmute that fear into a healthier fuel (like emotional fulfilment, or contribution to a bigger cause) that we're able to use discipline in conjunction with patience in order to truly see that striving for perfection was a pipe dream all along. Rather, Saturn nudges us towards realistic visions and goals that never required us to be perfect anyway.

Perfection

I've struggled with writing this book because of my perfectionism. Feeling like an imposter, wanting to sabotage the whole project along the way, to set it on fire. It can become hard to discern in our own heads who has the steering wheel. And most importantly, why. Why are they there to begin with? These things all become most apparent on the cusp of expansion, with our subconscious blocking our own success. It's our job to use this friction and turbulence wisely. To create a focused strength rather than let it derail us.

When I was fourteen, I was so uncomfortable in my body. I'd just got braces, which made me very self-conscious, and I didn't seem to have developed like the other girls in my year. I felt like I was this tiny little rake who would never feel desired. My dad would sing me this song in an attempt to make me feel better. Its lyrics were 'perfect hair, perfect teeth, we model ourselves on Normandie Keith. We're It girls.' Now, this was a harmless little limerick. However, I internalised this as an instruction. And through a variety of experiences during this time in my life, I started to believe that in order to be loved, I *had* to be perfect. I recounted the story to a friend not so long ago, who said something to me I'd never considered. He told me, 'Your dad didn't sing that to you because he wanted you to be perfect. He sang it because to him, you already were.'

Perfection as an instruction seeps into our world day to day, but I've realised that there's nothing less relatable than perfection. We're all fed a belief that being perfect guarantees an outcome, but it only causes us to stall. We think it'll absolve all the horrors of being a human being, but it's a complete illusion. The thing that really unifies us and connects us in the way we all truly desire is in fact what we seek to avoid through our perfection. It's our struggle and our pain. I believe it's how we alchemise our pain that brings both us and others joy. It's the awareness of both light and dark in the world and in ourselves, not denying or hiding from it. It's in owning all aspects of who we are. This is what we should aspire to achieve: alchemy.

My paralysing fear around music really reflected a fear around being truly seen and being vulnerable. The opposite of love isn't hate, it's indifference. There's a fine line between love and hate and we all know how quickly the coin can turn. Wherever we're most scared, wherever there's the most fear, go there. Follow that. Because beyond it is usually where the magic lies. Be courageous enough to go beyond the self and the ego. This is something I'm still trying to master.

Discipline

Self-discipline was one of my hardest lessons. It didn't come easily or naturally. It's a Saturnian principle and includes patience and perseverance. The fast fame *Made in Chelsea* days that came so easily didn't last. I remember when I was studying acting in New York, the landlord to my little

Avenue C rental apartment in Alphabet City was a man called Mike, who was Brooklyn born and bred. One evening while I was in the basement doing my laundry, he told me something I've never forgotten. He said each person has to spend the majority of one decade dedicating and hustling, striving for their dreams, and then they can spend the next decade enjoying it.

I was nineteen. I remember looking at him, perplexed by this idea of working hard, and thinking, not for me. In his gravelly Brooklyn drawl, he said, 'You don't get it now, kid, but one day you will.' He was right – I didn't get it then. But I sure do now. And a decade on, I think about it a lot, and I believe he was totally right.

Looking back, I wish I'd taken things more seriously then and taken on that advice. Then maybe my Saturn Return wouldn't have been so intense. I tried every shortcut in the book. I tried to cheat the game. But there are no shortcuts. Not really. Not if you want to build something that lasts.

If you want your house to be built on solid ground, you have to build the foundations first. For this reason, one's Saturn Return is often the moment when people really start grafting. It breaks things down so you can create something of meaning. It's the beginning of one's decade of dedication.

SUCCESS AND FAILURE

When our Saturn Return hits, we may begin to experience a sense of our own authority and also a release from restriction and expectations. Saturn's Return represents the ending of one chapter and the beginning of a new, forcing you to live more authentically. It begins a whole new phase of your life. Over this time, you start to consolidate all of your experiences, lessons and mistakes and take stock of your life so far. As you move forwards, you acknowledge your failures, but don't let them define your future. Use them as a map of your internal world for better understanding of self and as fuel to project you in the direction you wish to go. I'll say this many times in this book: it's crucial to know and play to our strengths, but it's just as advantageous to know our weaknesses, too.

To know success, we must first meet its counterpart: failure. For failure is where most of the lessons lie.

When our Saturn Return starts, we're often faced with a personal identity crisis, which can also be reflected in our career path. We're hoping our careers, romantic partnerships and sense of self will all have aligned by the time we're thirty, which in reality is a tall order. We need time to find out who we are and what we want to do in life. To uncover the inner workings of our psyche and what is truly in alignment.

One of the greatest tragedies is that we deny ourselves the things we love because of this idea that we have to have cemented who we are in this world by thirty. We get trapped in comparison – the ultimate thief of joy. But it doesn't matter what age you are when you start doing the work. It doesn't matter what age you are when you decide to change direction in life. And it doesn't matter what other people are doing!

We're living in a time where there are not only more options, but also more pressure than ever, with housing markets rising far quicker than our salaries. However, I believe these moments of rock bottoms and spiritual awakenings crystallise and develop our strategies for life. They force us to change course. It's within our lostness, our isolation that we're forced to discover ourselves. This might come from a dramatic ending, losing our job, hitting a dead end. Or perhaps we have created the perfect life, achieved all our goals and yet we are still unhappy. Realising we might have made the façade, but there's still an empty void within. Either way, we can begin to build again establishing our legacy over the next thirty years.

I used to be terrified of failing. So much so that for a large chunk of my twenties, I became so paralysed by fear of taking the wrong step that I took no step at all. People generally don't like talking about their failures because there's often a lot of shame attached to them. Our identities are so interwoven with what we do that we allow our failures to diminish our sense of self. Boxing them away in the attic, for no one to see. But failure is essential on the road to success and discovering our purpose – and that box is like a toolkit we need for our path, and we should treat it as such.

I've failed in business. I've failed in relationships. I've failed in friendship, family and so on. In my twenties, I agonised over these failures. As if each one of them somehow limited my experience and made me less than. But they actually expanded me. I just needed to reframe my perspective.

The bad business decisions I made, life choices, relationship breakdowns, family dramas, you name it, all gave me the necessary experiences for how *not* to do things. They invited me to go deeper into self-inquiry. And when I fail again, which inevitably I will, I will try to view that failure as an opportunity to adjust the sails rather than capsize.

Elizabeth Day, author and podcast host of *How to Fail* and the first ever guest on my podcast, *Saturn Returns*, perfectly demonstrates how unifying failure is and how rich it is in wisdom. The paradoxical experience is that you feel so much stronger for expressing your failures, which removes the shame. Failing gives us the sturdiness we need. As one of my heroes, Brené Brown, says in her TED Talk 'Listening to Shame', being open and vulnerable about our struggles and failures allows us to have greater bonds and deeper connections. It also creates the antidote to shame, which is empathy.

Quarter-life crisis, midlife crisis, personal crisis or Saturn Returns . . . whether or not you want to look at it astrologically or otherwise, there are certain moments in our life when people start to wake up and question the way they've been living. They feel like they're having some sort of existential crisis in the process. This can feel incredibly isolating and is often where we feel like we've somehow failed at the game of life. But it is just the awakening of our inner knowing.

To begin, we must learn to talk to each other – really talk. About what's bothering us, what we're struggling with and how we can better support one another. We live in such a world where we're trying to create and maintain a perfect image. But through sharing our problems and struggles, we can find solutions. We find community and we find connection. The truth is, the issues or problems that I feel are unique to me are probably things some of you might be experiencing. But when we struggle through anything in isolation, it's hard to recognise that these feelings are very normal, human and universal.

In my twenties, if I couldn't predict with certainty that I wouldn't fail, I didn't want to try. One of my podcast guests and friend, author and entrepreneur Steven Bartlett told me that when it comes to making tough decisions, sometimes you'll only be 51 per cent sure. But that's enough. Don't sit around and think about it: make a decision and take action. As someone who's a professional procrastinator (put that down to being a Libra rising), I've always really struggled when it comes to making decisions. I've always searched for 100 per cent certainty and according to Steven, this rarely exists.

'But what if you make the wrong decision?' I asked.

'Then fail fast,' he said.

This was almost revolutionary to me – we can never guarantee we aren't going to make a mistake. But sometimes we just have to take charge, take a leap of faith and be OK with our decision, whatever the outcome. Regrettably, I've spent way too much time sitting on the fence, agonising over every move. But looking back, I don't regret the things I went for or the chances I took, even if they didn't work out. I regret the things I didn't do. The chances I didn't take, the roads I never walked because I was too scared. It's far better to live with short-term disappointment than long-term regret. So do the things that scare you. Be brave, and if you fail, which you might, fail fast.

The business I started and failed at in my twenties allowed me to learn how to handle a business in my thirties. It enabled me to make smarter decisions when it came to ownership and building a team. Learning the 'hard way' meant that I didn't make the same mistakes the second time round. In a similar way, a shattering heartbreak in my twenties that I handled terribly gave me an example of what not to do in the midst of a break-up when I was thirty.

Maybe failing is the ultimate school of life? We can try

to avoid it, to hide from it. But then we'd never learn. A child only learns to walk by fumbling and falling again and again until it eventually gets it right. It doesn't judge itself for trying. I wish I'd spent less time in my twenties agonising over every hypothetical outcome. Less time berating myself in my failures. I have by no means mastered this, and I'm saying it to myself as much as to you. But we must loosen our grip on trying to control everything, trust a little in life and know it's not the enemy. The best things come in unexpected ways when we stop forcing and start trusting.

When we have a lack of trust, inversely that can cause us to subcontract our own authority. We lack trust in ourselves and in the Universe, and often fear taking responsibility. So we wait for it to be someone else's decision, handing over the keys to our kingdom. If we don't exercise our trust muscle, it'll never strengthen. By stepping into our own authority, we begin to cultivate experiences that over time build that muscle.

If you haven't been taking responsibility up until this point, don't panic. I definitely hadn't! This is a common Saturnian principle many must learn during this transition. At first it may feel foreign, but the Universe will keep putting challenges and obstacles in your path that are constant invitations for you to show up for yourself. It's not as clear- cut as pass or fail. It just comes round again in another form.

If you're alarmed by this, please don't worry. And if you're unhappy with where you are at in life, read on. Everything can be turned around, and the discomfort is simply an indicator that there's work to be done to get you back in alignment. It might require you to push beyond your comfort zone. But this is where the magic happens!

You have more courage than you know.
You just need the tools to access it.

Have a think now and jot down any big decisions you're struggling to make or any plans you're putting on hold unnecessarily. Think about what the first step might be to taking control of those situations. You'll be surprised by how simple those steps can be and how empowering it feels to make them.

For example, I might write:

I want to expand my brand, so I need to find the people who can help me do this and learn to delegate. I need to be more structured with my day and create clear parameters around expectations. I want to step more into the role of a leader, so I will need to demonstrate that by communicating to those around me, so they can show up to their fullest ability. Firstly, I can imagine what this would feel like, and visualise who I want to become so I can step into that role more fully.

Use this space to write your list:

When it comes to work and career, it's vital to get clear on what success means to you. It might mean the opportunity to take a sabbatical to allow you to travel. It might mean securing flexible hours to fit round a family. Or it might mean pursuing a dream you've had since you were a child. We don't all operate in the same way or want the same things, so why do we adopt one idea of success that involves a huge salary, an impressive title and a swanky office?

A great tool for accessing this and getting clear is listing the things that you want from your life. The things that define success for you. For me, these are freedom, flexibility, truth-seeking, authenticity, collaboration, personal growth and creativity. Once we've made peace with the inevitability of failure, we have to look more deeply into what success really means to us and how *we* define it. Not just what the world and media tell us it is. Not the movies about fast cars, mansions and flashy things.

What does success really mean to *you*? List what success looks like or feels like. Don't worry so much about the end goal or if it doesn't make sense in a career trajectory. By putting it out there, you'll have communicated to the Universe a clear message. It'll show you the next step to take, so pay attention. And a note: sometimes it's the things that come easiest to us, the path of least resistance that leads the way.

For example, I might write something along the lines of the following:

Success to me means living a life true to myself. With good friends, and a career that creates the freedom to travel and explore. It means not being beholden to anyone. Waking every day and feeling excited by what possibilities are around the corner. It's being financially comfortable. Being recognised in my field. And growing in wisdom.

HAPPINESS

When it comes to happiness, how much of our own lives do we let be dictated by society's conditioning? Perhaps outside expectations, parental figures casting their own experiences or failures onto us, social media. Even friendship groups can be incredibly limiting (if we're in the wrong ones). How much do our external influences narrate our life? I'd say for the majority, almost entirely.

I always thought I needed someone to tell me how to live my life, to give me permission to do certain things. And when you're someone who seeks approval and validation outside of yourself, you'll be sure to find a plethora of people who want to tell you how to live your life. (Just open any social media app.) Most of these individuals are just casting their own limiting beliefs onto you. Keeping up with the Joneses has a whole new meaning today. Instead, we're trying to keep up with the Kardashians.

Now your turn. List what success means to you:

_____

_____

_____

_____

_____

_____

_____

_____

_____

_____

_____

_____

_____

_____

_____

_____

You only have to open your phone to access how millions are sharing a highlight reel of their life. It can be incredibly discouraging. Social media isn't a healthy medium for measuring or identifying your success. It's too vast. Comparison is the thief of joy, and will be the death of your authentic creative output. We place too much importance on how to best advertise our lives rather than live them, and contrary to all the smiling faces, it's not making us happy.

The old methods or conditions we're often governed by are outdated. Don't just do what society or your parents or peers want from you. As Steven told me in our interview together, 'The biggest risk in life is living a life untrue to yourself.' You're not too old and you haven't left it too late. There are so many possibilities at your feet and we only ever get this one life. It's so worth it to go out there and seek your own path.

We've established that what success is to you might be totally different from what it is to me. But the reason we all chase 'success' is because we believe it'll make us one thing: happy. So when we talk about success, we're talking about our quest for happiness.

In this hedonistic lifestyle so many of us lead, we start out with perhaps humble aspirations. Once those are achieved, our goals get bigger. We hit the next milestone – the pay rise, the new car, the better job, the better partner – but we keep seeking. Along the way, we think to ourselves, when I get the next thing, then I'll be happy. But after the next thing, there's another thing and another and so on. As one's wealth increases, so does one's appetite for material things. Then we start comparing ourselves to people who have more than us, unable to outrun this feeling of falling short. This is the 'hedonic treadmill' and it never stops once you're on it.

In psychology, there are two main conceptions of happiness, and one is hedonic. Hedonic happiness stems back to the fourth century BC, when Greek philosopher Aristippus taught that the ultimate goal in life should be to seek and maximise pleasure. While I believe it is shifting, in Western culture, hedonic happiness is still very much championed as the ultimate goal. The second kind of happiness is eudaimonic happiness, which also dates back to the fourth century when Aristotle claimed that to live a life of happiness, one must live in accordance with one's virtues. Eudaimonia – from the Greek word *eudaimōn* meaning lucky, and *eu* plus *daimon* (spirit) meaning happy – is achieved through experiences of meaning and purpose. In other words, a life governed by reason and virtue. It's the individual's quest in this life to realise and fulfil their unique potential.

We need a blend of both hedonism and eudaimonism to achieve happiness. Sometimes after a rough day we need to indulge in the senses, eat, enjoy and be hedonistic. But on the whole, we need to move more in the direction of eudaimonia. This shift in psychology often occurs around your Saturn Return, where you crave authenticity and become more interested in personal growth rather than temporary fixes. As a result of social media, a great deal of focus is still on the exterior side of things, so this shift requires us to focus on nurturing our internal worlds rather than the external one.

When your internal world is watered, your external world will flourish.

I encourage you to start questioning why you're chasing certain things, whether it be a job, a house or a relationship. If it's for validation, which for many of us it is, it's important to understand that no amount of external validation will be enough if you don't validate yourself first. We can spend our energy creating the perfect facade. We can get that sports car and the glitzy things. But I found that most people I've met, especially during my time in LA, who had 'everything' weren't happy at all.

External pleasures will have no meaningful impact on your inner world if it hasn't been tended to, but if you nurture your mind and well-being, it'll light up your external world in a whole new way. When we nourish our internal worlds, our external world will flourish. In this capitalistic world that profits off insecurity and this perpetuating feeling of 'not enough-ness', it's a revolutionary act to be satisfied with your life. In fact, if you are, it's so rare, people might think you're completely mad.

Gratitude is really the key to happiness. I'm guilty of getting caught on the hedonic treadmill, but I have to catch myself and remember that the things that truly bring me joy are accessible to me at all times. When you really think about it, ask yourself when you were most happy. It probably wasn't when you bought that new car or those clothes – that happiness is a fleeting hit of dopamine. It was invariably in a moment when you were present in life's simple pleasures or in a moment of connection with someone you care about, or when you achieved something you didn't think was possible.

It isn't always easy, but every day I try to focus on what brings me true happiness and makes me feel most grateful. I've made a list of these things here and I invite you to list yours alongside:

Happiness is . . .

My morning tea	
Deep belly laughs with my best friends	
Cooking	
An act of kindness from a stranger	
Time to rest	
Walks in nature	

Part 3

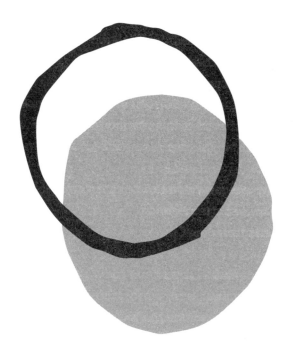

Matters of the Heart

Saturn's return really confronts us with the
fallacies in our self-confidence . . . it obligates us
to stop patterns of self-sabotage and thrive.
Africa Brooke

Noura's astrological insight:

*Although Saturn is often perceived as a cold planet, it isn't.
It's a humble planet. Rather, it has an energy that we possess
and that we all experience that's rooted in humility. In love,
especially when experiencing heartbreak around a Saturn
Return, the reason for our heartache will often be that the
person we were with wasn't truly who we thought they
were. Perhaps we had rose-coloured glasses on or maybe we
were continuously pouring energy into a relationship that
was draining us and holding us back in some way. Other
times, we could be the cause for this heartbreak, too.*

*We could have induced it by acting in a way that was
not only betraying them, but also ourselves. Betraying our*

boundaries and accepting behaviour that disempowered us. We could have told ourselves that we're ready for commitment when we're not. We could have convinced ourselves that we wanted a person to mark our whole checklist, then when we finally found this person, we're disillusioned and disappointed. This begs the question: Did we really know what we wanted?

Chances are, we didn't. And the heartbreak came when Saturn was Returning with a loving yet stern gaze. It saw that we weren't truly sure of this love or that the other wasn't truly sure what love meant for them. So, the true colours come to the surface and the relationship falls apart. For others, especially those who already had a healthy sense of boundaries in love, they tend to meet someone during their Saturn Return who might teach them all about a giving, enduring and generous type of love. Either way, when it comes to love, whichever major love event happens during Saturn's Return, it's nearly always for the best. No matter how heartbreaking it might have seemed, it came to free us from our limited perceptions of love. It expands our hearts and creates space for a love that can last the highs and lows of life.

As psychotherapist Esther Perel would say, 'Where should we begin?' I'm such a lover of love. As a Taurus sun and Libra rising, I'm twice ruled by Venus, and relationships have always taken centre stage in my life. Sometimes this has been my downfall. No matter how hard I try to shrink their importance into some kind of balance with the rest of my life, I'm a hopeless romantic at heart.

In my thirty odd years, I've had the privilege of experiencing many kinds of love, and although each relationship ended, not one was a failure. Each one taught me something different, gave me a different perspective on life, allowed me to soften in love and strengthen through heartbreak. They were mirrors reflecting back to me parts I couldn't see on my own that needed to be healed. I visited parts of myself I never knew existed, and I loved and was loved in return.

Matters of the heart can be a battlefield: tragic, messy, devastating, karmic, exhilarating, heart-pounding, intoxicating and wonderfully addictive. Love universally blinds and binds every soul with a heartbeat on the planet, and yet we know very little about it.

Saturn can have a devastating impact on our love life, because it often brings an abrupt and painful end. That was my experience, anyway, and in this chapter, I focus on Saturn's lessons in love. And man, oh man, there have been a few. But let's start at the beginning, shall we?

FIRST LOVE

I first fell in love when I was fifteen, during my Saturn opposition. I remember the feeling to this day. Cupid shot an arrow straight through the heart in an Earls Court nightclub when I saw a boy across the bar. And in that moment, my world stopped. I'll never forget it. This love, infatuation, whatever you want to call it, lasted for the best part of seven years. A whole Saturn season. Sure, there were romances and flings in between, but at the time, nothing compared to this. I adored him like it was my life's purpose.

We broke each other's hearts a few times – mine more than his. It was an on–off relationship over those years, more off than on, but that didn't mean I stopped loving him for one second. From school to university, through gap years and travelling, every summer we'd reunite in some serendipitous way and begin another chapter. As I went into the next phase of my life at twenty-one, the book closed. This love had taught me that love was flighty, inconsistent. Rarely present but always there. Available for fleeting moments, but for the most part out of reach. Even though we might not think about these early experiences, our subconscious has kept the score. I believe our Saturn Return calls us to revisit the past to make way for a different kind of future.

It wasn't until my mid-twenties that I went through the next big love chapter of my life. The all-consuming and debilitating kind that you willingly lose yourself in. The kind of love where the remedy and poison are one and the same, where you get trapped in the cycle of relapse and recovery. Mending simply to break all over again. I call it toxic love.

It was a relatively short-lived love affair; we were together for six months. No time at all considering the impact it had on me. We'd been set up through a friend who thought it might just be a bit of fun, but on the first night of meeting, we'd already said 'I love you.' Now if that doesn't spell disaster, I don't know what does. But this was very 'on brand' with me at the time. When you go from 0 to 100 miles an hour in seconds, you're bound to crash into a wall at some point. Which of course we did.

He was charming and charismatic and had danger written all over him. But after six months of manic highs and disastrous lows, my heart couldn't handle it anymore. The day it ended, I didn't want it to. In fact, it was the last thing I wanted. But all of my friends were screaming from the sidelines 'What are you doing?!' as I willingly entered the ring for another round and another knockout punch. Figuratively speaking, of course

In many ways, it was becoming an act of self-harm to stay. I was at Waterloo station, on my way to stay with my mum in the Isle of Wight, waiting for the train. We'd had another fight. I was distraught. It seemed every time it got better, something would go wrong again – wrong in the most imaginative ways. Like he was playing whack-a-mole with my emotions. We were either madly in love or at each other's throats and nothing in between.

I was exhausted and becoming a shadow of my former self. It was a sliding doors moment: the train came, the phone rang, the doors opened. He was begging me to go back to try to fix things for what felt like the thousandth time. But I knew I had to break this destructive cycle. I was chasing that initial high that was never quite the same. I stepped onto the train, tears streaming down my face. When I got to my mum's, I remember crying to her about how much it hurt. I'll never forget her reply: 'Love shouldn't hurt like this.'

The most painful part of this whole experience was knowing I'd abandoned myself by staying in a situation that wasn't loving. An act of abandonment like that is bad for you on a deeper level and creates a visceral pain. The pain of your heart betraying your soul. That love made me feel like I had to abandon myself to keep it, but when it becomes a choice between loving someone or losing ourselves, loving someone should never be synonymous with leaving ourselves behind.

Once we leave our own path to join someone else's, getting back on track becomes harder the further along you go. The road back looks long and empty, so we stay. We stay and we wrestle with reason, hoping that our hearts haven't betrayed us, or that we haven't betrayed our hearts. What we eventually come to learn through Saturn's guidance and with the help of astrology is that our paths are always uniquely our own. Saturn wants us to know we can maintain autonomy and personal sovereignty and also be in partnership with another. To create enough space for both people to have their independence while also nurturing healthy interdependency.

There are always indications of when this has gone off track. Saturn usually has a way of turning that 'wrong path' into quicksand to stop you in your tracks, to give you a moment to re-evaluate your decision. This can come in many forms. You may experience it physically through your body with anxiety, through a deep guttural knowing or through good old-fashioned rejection (or as I like to call it, God's redirection).

THE PERPETRATOR AND THE VICTIM

It took years to truly mend from the break-up I experienced in my mid-twenties. Part of the reason for that was that I went straight into another relationship and didn't give myself time to heal. I also took zero responsibility for the part I played. Instead, I created a narrative that made him the perpetrator and me the victim. In some ways, right now my ego is still shouting 'But that was true – he was!' But here's one of the most profound things I've learned in love: we all possess both. (NB: this excludes victims in abusive relationships.)

Rightness versus wrongness is corrosive in relationships. When we blame or shame another, we aren't looking at where we've been activated or where we're projecting because it feels too painful and we don't know what to do with that pain. It's easier to villainise the other person, but in this process, we often neglect to see the wisdom in the pain or the opportunity to grow. When a relationship ends, there's always an opportunity to deepen our relationship with ourselves. When one love goes, does self-love remain? The problem is, we often seek the love we wish we could give ourselves. It took me until after my Saturn Return to truly realise this. The more I looked for love outside of myself, the less I found it.

Once I began my spiritual path, I started to recognise my patterns. I could intellectualise them, but Saturn challenged me to put the theories into practice. My Saturn Return fell exactly over the period of a relationship and ended almost the same day the relationship ended. When we're betrayed, we can easily feel victimised, and understandably so. It brings to the surface all of our fears about ourselves and it can make us question our worth.

When my world as I knew it fell apart in a flash, my self-esteem was hanging in the balance. I was at a crossroads: Would this break me, or make me? All the old feelings of inadequacy that I'd experienced in my youth came up, particularly the feeling that I wasn't enough. But I knew the woman I was on the precipice of becoming *was* enough.

During that time, I felt very aware of the inner child in me, and I spoke to her and soothed her. In that awareness, I felt a sense of liberation, like I was at the head of the table with all the different parts of me.

One of my favourite quotes is from author Glennon Doyle in her book *Untamed*: 'There is no such thing as one-way liberation.' I remind myself of this daily. What's not meant for one person is ultimately not meant for the other. If it liberates one, it also liberates the other. You deserve a love that chooses you fully. Don't settle for half love. Trust this. It's the truest thing.

When I interviewed *Create the Love* podcast host and human connection specialist Mark Groves for the *Saturn Returns* podcast, he mentioned American philosopher and author Sam Harris's book *Free Will*, in which he explains how we project our own free will onto other people. But If you traded lives with someone cell for cell, experience for experience, you'd do everything they've done.

When we say that someone has a choice they didn't make, we say it from our own privilege, our own advantage, our own space. I've always been someone who tries to put myself in someone else's shoes in an attempt to understand their behaviour. I've realised over time that this is often futile, because sure, maybe I would have behaved differently in that situation. But we can sometimes use this to take a stance of superiority over one another, professing 'I'd *never* have done what they did.' Sure you wouldn't, because guess what? You aren't them. But if you were, you would have.

I believe our demands from relationships have changed, but our education around them hasn't. We want a deep level of intimacy, but we're often unwilling to look at our own less than perfect behaviour in order to secure it. We underestimate the heavy lifting it requires. Love requires work, understanding and patience. And if I had to say one thing that'll define the success of a relationship, it's not the absence of conflict, it's how well the conflict is handled and navigated.

What I have learned is that when something happens in a relationship – a fight or a throwaway comment – that makes your system go into shutdown mode, defensive mode or overdrive, you need to get curious. What's triggered you, and why? Next, allow space. Sometimes we need to go off for a moment, an hour or even a day to calm down after our emotional state has been dysregulated. Finally, ask your partner for time to talk. Schedule it if necessary. Then communicate what came up for you. For example, 'When you said this, it brought up this for me . . . And I wanted to share that with you so we can work through it together.'

This is acknowledging and owning your own part, your own wound, and not projecting it onto the other person. You're allowing the other person to participate in your healing, rather than making them out to be the cause of your pain. This will create deeper trust, as you'll have a new and powerful experience to refer to when you get triggered again. Communication met with vulnerability is the recipe for the right outcome. It'll defuse the conflict. And will stop your ego from sabotaging something potentially great.

The paradox and complexity of being able to hold two truths – to make space for the other person's experience without it invalidating your own – is crucial. How can we listen more, judge less, soften more, defend less? When handling conflict, what's the quickest way to win and work through it? Simple: it's to put down your weapon first.

This is especially hard in the demise of a relationship, where we speedily jump to all the things *they* did wrong. How they let us down, where they fell short, how they hurt us, etcetera. How liberating would it be to be grateful instead? What did they show you about yourself? What's the experience taught you? How can we take radical responsibility for ourselves and our hearts?

The truth is, we never know what someone else's experience is. Not truly. We like the safety in thinking we do, but as we all know too well, people can surprise us. The burden of contempt in or out of a relationship weighs heavy on the heart. Chastising another doesn't elevate oneself. Controlling another doesn't give us safety. Saturn taught me to let go of blame and control. It taught me that this idea of 'better than' or 'too good for' is an illusion, a false security. The intricacies of why two people work together and another two don't are beyond the realms of our comprehension.

TRUST YOUR GUT

How do we know if it's right? The simple answer is this: if it's right, you'll know. If it's wrong, you'll be confused.

Embarrassingly, in the past I've found myself in the midnight hours searching Google for a reason to stay in situations that had run far past their sell-by date, trying to justify the unjustifiable. Lost in the abyss of a Reddit thread with a sea of other women doing the same. Not a good place to be, and it's a fairly good litmus test of knowing when it's time to move on.

I always think about the fact that as human beings, we have language and logic, and we bend that logic according to our stories. For example, an animal will instinctively sense danger, have a physical reaction and run away. We, on the other hand, will sense danger, have a physical reaction, get the girls over, drink some wine and convince ourselves it's a good idea.

So, forgive yourself for staying when you should have left. Speak your truth unapologetically, choose yourself, and know that those who value you and can hold space for you in safety will stay and those who can't will go. Know that you can't guarantee the one you *think* you want will show up for you. The victory is in the process of showing up for yourself, regardless of the outcome. Don't be afraid to lose them; be afraid to lose yourself. The irony is we go into relationships asking for unconditional love armed with a long scripture of conditions. We must be wary of our own hypocrisy! Unconditional love doesn't mean unconditional tolerance. We have to have our non-negotiables when entering a relationship. This allows us to discern who is in alignment with us, and filters out those who are not. For example, mine are as follows:

- A kind heart

- Self-awareness

- On a spiritual path, an openness to see the world differently to learn new things

- Ability to hold space for me emotionally

- Integrated and grounded in his masculinity

- Encourages me to speak my truth

- Sexually compatible and strong sexual connection

- Can show up in hard times

- Must be extremely silly and playful, too.

This would be a wonderful moment for you to think about what your real non-negotiables are and make note of them on the page opposite.

When we love someone with all these non-negotiable qualities, we have to accept that they still might not do all the little things exactly the way we want. Or they might have different ways of communicating love than how we're used to receiving it. Looking into our love languages can be helpful in understanding these differences in the ways we give and receive love. If you're curious, you can simply google 'Love Language Test' to discover what's most powerful for you, be it touch, words of affirmation, quality time, acts of service or gifts.

Remember, we're all unique beings who ultimately all have our own fears and insecurities, and we all want to be loved. We love in spite of our partner's flaws and we have to accept them wholly. But if the differences are too big to ignore, we have to understand that sometimes, loving someone means letting them go.

Podcast guest and award-winning author, teacher and dreamworker Toko-pa Turner's book *Belonging* contains a chapter that really struck a chord with me, and it's something we don't practise but I believe we should. It's the art of 'leaving well'. It's generally been my experience to cut off contact when a relationship ends, and don't get me wrong, sometimes this is the only option. But I remember reading

My list of non-negotiables are as follows:

_____

_____

_____

_____

_____

_____

_____

_____

_____

_____

_____

_____

_____

_____

_____

_____

_____

this book and thinking about how many times I've shut things down and dramatically cut off all communication. Probably as an act of self-preservation, but mainly out of an inability to state my needs and perhaps an attempt to regain control.

We often talk about closure in a relationship as this final chapter that allows us to find meaning in experience. But it's not always possible, as it requires two people to come together and see each other's points of view, and hold space for one another, even in the demise. If it can be executed in the right way, it can be a beautiful ritual – albeit a sad one – that invites healing and honours the grief.

Love is a container and if it fractures through conflict, it'll either deepen or break. How we show up for conflict is important – in or out of a relationship. We can't force another to do it with us, but we can show up anyway. Leaving well means we behave in a way that honours our integrity and shows respect for the relationship. This is what Saturn is all about – living by and in accordance with one's values. Just as we should live with integrity, we should leave with it, too.

Our fragile egos get in the way of our connections and as we become more vulnerable, we fear too much is at stake, so we stonewall, gaslight, criticise or shut down. We repeat the same patterns again and again because we were never taught how to show up differently. Communication is the key to a healthy relationship, but it's a learned skill. With

Saturn being in my third house (house of communications) this has always been a big challenge.

We have to take full responsibility for how we show up – what our subconscious biases are around relationships and people – and address them head-on. We always say looking for love or finding love, but I believe, like one of my favourite teachers Mark Groves says, that we *create* the love.

MENDING A BROKEN HEART

Noura's astrological insight:

In astrology, Saturn finds harmony in the signs ruled by Venus. Venus brings love, art, comfort, luxury, friendships and knowledge to our lives. Venus is the goddess of love, also known as Aphrodite in Greek mythology. Being the stoic planet that it is, Saturn has an affinity for Venus. It admires its ability to devote itself completely to all that beautifies, discerns and unites. At the core, they have very similar values. Therefore, when it comes to the topic of love, Saturn supports this completely.

But in its support, it can be extremely stoic. Saturn loves 'love', yes, but it certainly doesn't believe in the notion of self-serving love. It supports devoted, mature, enduring relationships and things of beauty. So leading up to one's Saturn Return, it can sometimes be shocking how a rela-

tionship we thought was just 'perfect' turns out to have been unsustainable and therefore not 'enduring'.

Through the brutal awakening of this fact, Saturn tries to protect us. Both our hearts and our vulnerability. And it invites us to mature and to treat ourselves in the way only a self-loving person could: with complete devotion and commitment. In doing so, anything that makes us stray us from this state of mind tends to fall out of our lives. Sometimes by erosion and at other times by sudden events that lead to confusion.

This can be heartbreaking, but – and this is the Saturnian silver lining – it offers a clean slate. We're nudged or, if we're stubborn, forced to change so that we may walk a more aligned path where self-love and self-sovereignty reign supreme. It won't happen all at once, for in true Saturnian way, we're asked to be patient, which is the signature of maturity (ask any Capricorn- or Saturn-dominant person). It isn't all doom and gloom, though. Some people meet their life partner or enter a legalised commitment during their Saturn Return. It all depends on the space we've created in our lives to be able to receive a love that's fair and just and giving and enduring, the way Saturn meant for us to experience love all along.

During your Saturn Return, break-ups are incredibly common. This is because we go through such huge shifts as individuals that we often outgrow the relationship in order to get into alignment with our true selves. The break-ups can be particularly brutal and unexpected, because Saturn doesn't like to mess around. You thought everything was fine and rosy, and then *bam!* As if from nowhere you're single again.

Break-ups are like a death. And as with the aftermath of any death, we'll experience grief.

Often, people try to move on to someone else quickly in an attempt to bypass this pain. Which is a bit like putting a plaster on a bullet hole; it might be a temporary fix, but it won't stop the bleeding. You have to let it breathe in order to heal. I truly believe that you have to honour a relationship by giving yourself space and time in the aftermath. You also don't want to fall into the trap of the rebound, diving head first into a relationship with the first person you meet.

Time is no measure for love. There's no fixed duration for its healing, either. I always say when asked how long it takes to get over a heartbreak, how long is a piece of string? I've been with people just a number of weeks, yet it's taken me years to get over them. Others I've been with for a number of years and it's taken me weeks to get over them. There's no rhyme or reason to it.

What I see happening is when we move too soon, we find someone who possesses all the things the previous partner lacked. So, if our previous partner was clingy, we might jump to someone who's distant (and we realise that actually, those things are annoying, unsuitable and incompatible with us, too.) It's a reaction to the fact we haven't healed or processed our experience, so we're plastering over the wound with another human being.

Often, fragments of our past relationships are carried with us and brought into our next relationship. If left unattended ,we often repeat the same cycles and it becomes hard to differentiate between past hurt or trauma and intuition. Being aware is the first step. Second is when we feel safe and comfortable with the person we're dating, we can share our experience. This doesn't have to be loaded. You can just let them know how certain behaviours might trigger you and invite a conversation about how to navigate this when it happens.

Historically, when I've been triggered or felt threatened in some way, I shut down so fast that Fort Knox would be easier to get into. Now, I bring it to the table. I share where my mind has gone, even if it's gone to the craziest of places! This diffuses its power, stops me from spiralling and spinning out, and allows my partner to reassure me. Obviously, you need a partnership where it's safe to do so, but by doing this, we slowly sweep out the remains of whatever hurt we experienced before and build a healthy foundation of trust in its place.

Love doesn't chase. If it comes, let it come. If it goes, let it go.

So, how do we move on from someone effectively? And how does Saturn's Return affect our break-ups? The grief we experience when a relationship ends is, more than anything, for the future we envisioned for ourselves. When we meet someone, we attach so many expectations to them about how our lives are going to intertwine and futures unravel together. So when a break-up happens, we have to detach ourselves from that imagined reality.

A large part of it is a fantasy, because our future is never really known, but as human beings we enjoy the idea that it is. The thought of having a blank canvas to start over is so daunting for some that they stay in a relationship far beyond its expiry date, simply out of fear of the unknown. It can be immensely painful. But break-ups can be rocket fuel to personal development and growth. I know what it's like to feel so certain it was right that you just can't let go, but I'm telling you: if it were right, it wouldn't have fallen apart. And soon enough, you'll be grateful that it did.

Why not take this moment to make a list of lessons you've learned from a break-up? This kind of thinking encourages us to keep growing and reminds us that we always come out the other side stronger. My list of lessons is long, but the one that comes to mind first is the following:

Over to you. Use this space to list what you've learned:

_____

_____

_____

_____

_____

_____

_____

_____

_____

_____

_____

_____

_____

_____

_____

**I trust in the Universe and its divine timing.
I know that what is meant for me, will not pass
me by. Even through heartbreak, I know I will
mend and love and be loved again.**

The heart and the body don't understand break-ups. That's why it's like a death. Your body doesn't know the difference between you having to part ways with someone and never seeing them again out of choice or circumstance. It just feels the void left by their absence.

If you're going through something like this right now, I see you and I feel your pain. I know it, truly. Those first mornings you wake up without them, unsure whether or not it was some cruel nightmare, until your new reality seeps in. To know you'll never spend another Sunday with them or do all the little things you did together that built the foundations of your love is crushing. All the little idiosyncrasies about them that you loved, because it made them them. I know how painful that is. I won't try to belittle it by giving some quick-fix heartbreak recovery crash course. But I also know that no matter how deep the pain, it's evidence of how deeply you loved, for all things run even.

Love should always be celebrated. It's one of the great and cruel paradoxes of it all – you can't know the depths of love without risking pain and heartbreak. And the deeper you go, the deeper the blow. But we do it anyway, because it's worth it. We can feel disconnected when a break-up happens, where everything is thrown upside down and uncertain, Simultaneously, we can also feel our most connected to ourselves. Among the heartbreak and the grief comes a choice. Do we marinate in this pain, overly identify with it, allow it to victimise us, or do you use it to re-empower ourselves?

When I went through my break-up during my Saturn Return, I initially attempted to bypass my own pain to be helpful to my ex. I tried to be strong for him and I overly spiritualised the whole experience, perhaps as I wasn't ready to address the anger or betrayal I felt. It was easier to play the healer than begin my own healing.

Fortunately, I was seeing a therapist at the time, who had created a steady foundation for me over the previous six months. This meant I was equipped with the tools not to fall into destructive old patterns of behaviour.

She did ask me one day, 'Are you angry?'

'Not really,' I said as I gave some overly intellectualised answer for why he behaved the way he did and how it had nothing to do with me.

To which she replied, 'You know, it's OK to be angry.'

The truth was I wasn't sure how to access my anger or my grief. I thought I'd fall apart if I did, because ultimately, I was still in love. In accepting the anger and grief, I'd also have to accept the end. Which at the time I wasn't ready to do.

Saturn's lessons in love are simply to let you know if your relationship is out of alignment with your true self.

If you are in the depths of heartache and going through a break-up, keep going, as I can promise you there will be light at the end. If you can even try to say 'Thank you' to the Universe, if you can be just as grateful for the pain as the love, it'll guide you to something so much greater. You have to believe that what's meant for you won't pass you by. The pain will become alchemised and you'll know yourself better. You'll even be able to love a little deeper, a little softer, a little braver.

I acknowledge that my twenties were spent shapeshifting in matters of the heart and arguably, all matters of my life. My Saturn Return taught me how to remain anchored in myself and not morph into some other version to suit someone else. It also allowed me to consider the possibility that a relationship isn't synonymous with having to change or alter myself. That, possibly, I could be loved just as I am.

You can't say the wrong thing to the right person.

I believe that we have many connections in life and many soulmates, some romantic, some platonic. People will come into our lives, creating an inflection point that alters the course of our fate. I believe every connection we experience should be celebrated and valued. Even if it lasts nothing more than a day. Even if it hurts like hell. If in the midst and the madness of love our hearts get broken, rather than berate the other for its demise, pinning its failure on their shortcomings, unable to acknowledge that they're a match for our own, instead we must learn to pick ourselves up and dust ourselves off. To pull down the drawbridge, get back into the arena and be brave enough to love again.

The problem with love is we want to contain it. To keep it and own it. But love cannot be contained. It's not to be kept or owned. It must remain untamed, mercurial and effervescent, its potency lies in the fact that it might disappear. You can't experience the depths of love and bypass the possibility of pain. That's the magic – that on the precipice of love, pain is always on the other side.

Much like all things in life, it runs even. This modern idea of completion from another is disempowering, because another person should never complete you. Real love is walking your own path in tandem with someone else's. Sometimes you'll go off track, sometimes you'll fall over. At times you'll be going at different paces and maybe you'll end up going in different directions. Ultimately, that's OK, and it doesn't diminish how much you loved or how deeply you felt.

So, if you're going through a break-up or looking to meet someone, I recommend that you meditate on it. Journal about the kind of person you want to call into your life and then get clear on what you're letting go of – what's no longer welcome in your life anymore. We can often hold someone from the past in such high regard as a protective mechanism to stop ourselves from being seen and vulnerable with somebody new.

In my weaker moments in the midnight hours, I used to catch myself lusting over the coulda, woulda, shouldas of the past. A story that would take me out of my present reality, which sometimes felt better than sitting in the space in between love. An extremist by nature, I've never been fond of neutrality, but it was a very Saturnian lesson for me to be able to sit rooted in reality and be OK with whatever that looked like.

As tempting as it is to get out the tiny violin and start replaying the pain and the heartache, and start ruminating over why they were the one who got away, instead try getting used to the space. Be OK with it. If possible, be excited by it. I know this can feel like a terrifying thing, as we're programmed to panic, especially post-thirty, about being single, manically going through our phone book seeking out lost loves and ghosts of the past. But honestly, do you really need to rush the decision to spend potentially the rest of your life with the wrong person? Take your time when it comes to matters of the heart. Because it matters!

Life, my friends, is a bit like a maze. Although we like to think of it as a straightforward trajectory, from a to b, the Universe has other plans, and Saturn comes in like a wrecking ball to throw you completely off course. But all those detours are part of the experience that makes it so much more enriching. I encourage you to say thank you to the

Universe for its guidance and let yourself go with the flow. You might not get what you *think* you want, but you'll get exactly what you need. Saturn isn't out to get you, but it'll strip away what isn't meant for you. In its place, it'll put something far greater than you could ever have imagined. Saturn wants you to take it slow, so take your time.

Remember that if someone can't contain all of you, if they don't understand the language of your soul that's beyond speech or human measure, if you didn't fit into their arms, it's not because they're too good or bad, or because you're too much or too little. It's because maybe they aren't meant to hold you at all. Liberate yourself and them, because the right person will fit without question. They'll breathe life into the words that only your soul understands. The right person will read you like they wrote the book. Wait for them.

**Love should never be rushed.
You're worth the wait.**

TRIUMPHANT PLATONIC LOVE

Noura's astrological insight:

Saturn naturally co-rules the eleventh house. The eleventh house is the house of network circles and friendships that are encouraging, lasting and supportive of your life goals and biggest dreams

It's often during Saturn's Return that we'll discover the friends who truly are supportive of us and those who aren't. Our friendship circle starts to reflect our healthier self-esteem and our more mature outlook on life. Unfortunately, this can mean having to let go of friendships with those who no longer seem to want to be part of our lives. At this stage, though, we learn so much about what a healthy friendship means. And although we might go through some loneliness during that time, unknowingly, we're almost always setting the foundation for friendships that start out slowly but tend to last through the next major milestones of our lives.

Besides friendships, we start to improve our networking skills – Saturn Return is the ideal time to start networking or to start exploring friendships in different social situations. The more eclectic or outside our natural comfort zone, the better. It's a time that encourages us to challenge our definition of normal, which in turn will reflect in the friendships we make and keep for a long time.

Triumphant platonic love. This one I didn't see coming. I've always been someone who had one best friend while growing up, one with whom I was joined at the hip. There was Grace from age seven to twelve, Humaira from twelve to fifteen and Tally from fifteen to twenty-eight (probably my longest relationship to date). Tally is still one of my closest and dearest friends, but during my Saturn Return, a lot of friendships shifted.

I found this incredibly hard. No one tells you about break-ups in friendships. The sorrow, the sadness. But friendships can often be the great loves of our lives. Looking back, I know all three of them were. Perhaps there aren't as many novels written about them, or films made. But true friendships are worth their weight in gold. True friendship lasts the test of time. They may transform into something new as life takes you in different directions, but they're always there.

During our Saturn Return, we're called to re-establish our values and consequently, the dynamics in our friendships change. It's hard because we want to stay the same for the sake of friendship, so things can continue as they were. But often we get a calling to go into the wilderness. To seek outside what we know, to venture off into the unknown. It can feel like a no man's land. You're no longer who you used to be, but you aren't sure who you are yet, either. You've outgrown those around you, but you're afraid that the right people won't find you and that you'll be alone.

When I had author Ruby Warrington on the podcast, we

talked about fitting in and belonging. How when faced with a choice between authenticity and belonging, we'll sacrifice our authentic truth to fit in, even in the wrong places, and often compromising our integrity along the way. This has been an adaptation and a means for survival. Historically, we've always needed a tribe or community to survive, but fitting in and belonging are actually opposites of each other.

The journey to belonging means belonging to ourselves first. It means accepting and loving ourselves first. In this modern digital world in which we live, we often place more value on being liked than on actually liking ourselves. I know this to be true of myself in the past and I felt this intensely during my Saturn Return. I'd oscillate constantly between people-pleasing and stepping into the direction of my truth, but the fear and isolation that came with it scared me so much that I'd return to old habits, behaviours and people I'd outgrown but felt safe with simply because they were familiar. When both options seem painful, we'll choose the familiar pain. Better the devil you know.

Eventually, the pain of staying the same and staying small starts to outbalance the fear of the unknown. I describe it as a self-inflicted exile, a necessary initiation into our becoming and our true belonging.

I was twenty-seven when I went through this shift. I kept having this specific vision of myself standing by the window of a house, wearing a soft pale peach-coloured dress. The house I was in was built to my exact liking and taste. It stood tall and alone. There was a long, winding road leading to it and I, as I was, was standing at the beginning of that road. Looking down the uninviting and lonely terrain towards this version of me. But I knew that version of me was my future self and that I had to walk this path to get there. There was no way around it – I had to go through it.

My mother always says, 'The loneliness you can feel when with the wrong person far outweighs the loneliness of being alone.' And I completely agree. My loneliest moments have been in a relationship that wasn't right or standing in the middle of a crowded room but feeling unseen. Equally, I've travelled to the other side of the world by myself and never felt less alone in my life. We are first and foremost relating to the self, so being alone doesn't necessarily mean you'll be lonely.

When you journey inwards, and focus on liking yourself, rejection won't derail you. Pay more attention to how your life feels, rather than how it looks to others. The richness of having a few friends who truly adore you is everything. It's far better to be celebrated and loved by a few in truth than the world for a lie.

A lot of people message me about struggling with this, because during our Saturn Return or any sort of transition in life, for that matter, we often have to walk this path of solitude. And as we do, friendships or relationships will go. The fear that the right people won't find you is understandable, but I promise – it's nothing more than a fear.

I can't tell you exactly how, because it's going to be unique to you. But as you step more and more into your truth, they just will. People will show up in expected ways. You'll feel a calling to reach out to someone from the past, or a desire to start talking to someone in a yoga class. Follow the intuitive pings as they come. Be brave enough to go to things alone that are in line with who you are today. I personally believe that being your authentic self and truly loving that person is the best way to attract someone who really connects with you. Call it the law of attraction or finding someone with the same frequency, if you like, but it all comes down to trusting in who you really are and not being afraid to share that with others.

After my big Saturnian break-up, I decided to go to Australia. From the first time I went to Australia when I was ten, it was like falling in love. At this point, I was looking for a sign for what to do, where to go, and Australia, a place I consider my spirit home, was just the ticket. I went for three weeks on my own over Christmas. I did yoga every day and I went to restaurants on my own with a book my only companion. I even spent most of Christmas Day on my own. I spent time with friends I'd made from when I lived there in my twenties, I walked for hours and I meditated. I read books on astrology and every day, I repeated the following mantra to myself: 'If all I do is heal, then that is enough.'

As I flew home, I felt so full. My heart was bursting with love. Love I'd given myself. Love I felt from being reunited with my spirit home and friends I hadn't seen in a long time. Love from the kindness of strangers. Looking back, I could never have predicted the series of events that unfolded over those few months and how they were going to shape me.

Just two months later, I started my company, Saturn Returns. A month after that, we launched the podcast. After the first episode aired, I received a message from a girl called Zoe who worked at Orion, a division of Hachette, the publishing house. It said how much she loved the concept of Saturn Returns and she asked whether or not I'd ever thought about writing a book. As Noura (our *Saturn Returns* resident astrologer) said at the time: 'Caggie, it's called Orion. It's written in the stars.'

Of course, we can't all head for Australia whenever we need this kind of grounding in ourselves, so I've learned to bring that peace to me, even when I'm at home in my usual routine. Meditation, yoga, walking and positive self-talk are practices I incorporate every week in some form, and they're my way of showing love to myself and giving myself a sense of belonging.

Use the space on page 162 to list the practices you use to come home to yourself and show yourself some love. It might be that you're not in the practice of showing up for yourself in this way, so if something comes to mind that you'd like to start incorporating into your routine, put it in your calendar and start as soon as possible.

Some of my favourites are:

- Long nature walks without my phone so I can be present with myself and all that is around me.

- Pulling tarot or inner compass cards to get some guidance when I am feeling stuck or ungrounded.

- Breathwork for regrounding or unearthing old emotions I need to shift.

- Spending quality time with friends.

The end of the relationship that was the end of my Saturn Return taught me I could always call on my practices to reground me. From that moment, I looked after myself consistently both physically and mentally through therapy and yoga. I embraced a more sober lifestyle and said yes to invitations and opportunities that I'd normally have shied away from. I remained open to the possibilities that life was going to throw at me, making new and exciting friends in the process.

At this time, I met my best friend Kelly, whom I now couldn't imagine my life without. I was introduced to her by our mutual friend Farleigh and it was platonic love at first sight. We talked for hours and hours. Just as rare as it is to have a connection romantically with someone that's

How do you come home to yourself?
Use this space to list the practices that you
can always call on wherever you are:

_____

_____

_____

_____

_____

_____

_____

_____

_____

_____

_____

_____

_____

_____

_____

_____

_____

so instant, this felt like that with a friend. It was like the rotational door of the Universe – one love left my life, but almost immediately in its absence came another. It was a different kind of love, but it's been just as profound.

I learned that loving yourself first will ground you at your core. I realised the value in all these esoteric things I'd been dipping my toe into and how I could always call on them to connect me back to myself. I had the greatest couple of months of my life and things continued to get better.

The most painful break-up acted like some sort of rocket fuel that got me off my arse and I just said to myself: no more playing it safe, no more playing it small. Starting the *Saturn Returns* podcast was one of the best things I ever did. Not just for my professional life, but also for my personal one. It's allowed me to connect with people from all walks of life – other like-minded free thinkers like myself. I've met some of my best friends now through interviewing them, like moon mentor and author Kirsty Gallagher, and consultant and coach Africa Brooke, who were both guests on the show – both of whom I now can't imagine my life without.

We value friendships that hold history, for they're rich in experience. Having known someone at different stages of their life is such a privilege, but meeting someone who totally aligns with who you are today and where you're going, who can call you out on your own shit but would also go to war for you – that's something to treasure.

The friendships I've developed since have filled my cup to the point where I rarely ever feel lonely. I know I have people who will be there for me when I need them. The power of platonic love has been such a wonderful thing over the last few years. We spend so much time worrying about finding our person or 'the one' but actually, the greatest loves of our life might be right in front of us – our best friends. They'll be there to help us mend when we're breaking, and they'll pick up the pieces and put us back together again. Treasure them.

Part 4

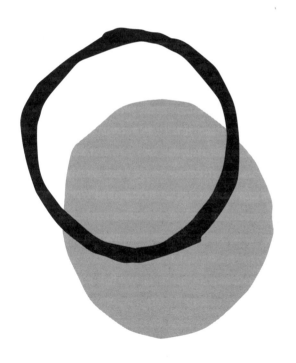

Self-Worth and Personal Sovereignty

We are taught that belonging is a static place of attainment that many of us will spend our whole lives searching for and we think well, if I keep looking for it, if I keep going into the further and further reaches I will finally find that place and I will recognise it and it will recognise me and we will live happily ever after in this state of unquestionable belonging but what I discovered was one of the key things that came through this work, was that belonging is not static at all but a dynamic process.

Toko-pa Turner

Noura's astrological insight:

It's interesting to note that someone with a prominent Saturnian influence in their chart (Saturn placed in the first, fourth, seventh or tenth house – or someone with a lot of Capricorn/Aquarius placements) struggles most with self-

worth and the recognition of personal sovereignty. The reason for this is that in its immature influence, Saturn can express itself in the form of authority figures during childhood and teenage years. Somehow, these then chip away at our self-confidence. It encourages a notion of excessive humility and diminishment of ego. So, although we might respect authority figures while growing up, we secretly also resent them for their strong and stifling influence on our personal freedom. In turn, we act out during our first Saturn opposition (age sixteen) by rebelling, or we further submit to authorities and the rules of those we deem to know better.

In its higher expression, at Saturn's Return, we're invited to rethink authority and what it means to us. Then we're nudged to contemplate where we've given over our own authority out of habit or subconscious submission. Later, as we perform the inner work, we'll awaken to the realisation that we do have a choice. We have free will. Although there's merit in honouring those who came before us, there's oppression in freely giving away our authority and in doing so, indirectly diminishing our sense of self-worth.

Authority figures serve to guide and when they try to enslave us by imposing restrictive ideas that are rooted in a need to control, we must set boundaries and demonstrate our own governance over our free will, our bodies, our choices. We must express our own authority and step into personal sovereignty. The more we do this, the easier it'll become. And hopefully, when it's our turn to guide those who need it, we *won't misuse it. Rather, we'll honour it and remind those who are younger of their value and their own sovereignty.*

Our self-worth should never live anywhere except inside our own heart and mind. The relationship we have with ourselves is the most important one we'll ever have, but we're often programmed to believe that our worth lives outside of us, and that romantic relationships are the most important ones in our lives. Many of us have been guilty of meeting someone and abandoning all the other components of our lives that bring us happiness and fulfilment.

While I was growing up, boys were the centre of my universe. But let's say your life is like a pie chart, and within said pie you have your friendships, your hobbies, your family, your career and your romantic/life partner. So many people (myself included) end up with a pie chart that's completely out of balance. When romance comes along, the romantic section takes up most of the space and those other slices get smaller, less valuable, less important, sometimes eradicated completely as a result.

We often measure our investment in someone by how much we like them, neglecting the crucial element of reciprocity, making ourselves completely available and malleable, demoting our other plans or commitments to ourselves and with our friends. We're so conditioned to eagerly await being taken off the shelf, as if our completion, our wholeness as human beings depends on it. This is a flawed mindset and we all need to outgrow it – you were born complete. It's just that the world has told you otherwise.

Over time, societal norms have created this belief that women are only as valuable as the men who pick them, but your romantic life is only a segment of what's going to make you happy. The concept that this one person is going to fulfil your needs, desires and wants while also filling that missing void inside you is part of the problem with modern love. A relationship, especially at its early stages, needs nourishment and attention, but with equal measure. As do your friends, your career and your family, and so do you. Make a conscious effort to keep those pieces even. Remember, you are also doing the choosing, not just being chosen. Cultivate a life that you're in love with independently from a partner. This is how you build self-worth and sovereignity over your life.

A lot of women message me through social media panicking about being single. Women of all ages. Some only twenty-seven or -eight. As If society at large is going to discard them for their single status post-thirty. I categorically refuse to prescribe to this narrative. I think it's toxic and ultimately untrue. No woman or man should ever be made to feel inferior for being single. Believing this only makes people settle for way less than they deserve.

Your relationship status should be the *least* interesting

thing about you. The social hierarchy of singletons, those in relationships and those who are married is based on a time where a woman's worth was little more than an exchange for security. Where a woman's survival and social status was dependent on it. I find the way people still view this perplexing. The way we congratulate women for finally getting chosen, disproportionately to how we congratulate men.

Although this might be disappointing news to some, we aren't living in the world of Jane Austen. It also makes single people have low self-worth when they should be feeling a million dollars. Dismantling this whole structure was so liberating for me. Luckily, my family has always been incredibly supportive of whatever I want to do with my life, and I have never felt pressure from them to settle down or have children. But of course I do have family friends whose first question is 'Are you married yet?'. Even before they've asked me how I am. It doesn't bother me; it shouldn't bother you. As the singer Cher famously said when her mother asked her if she was ever going to settle down and find a rich man. To which she iconically replied, 'Mom, I am a rich man.'

DISCOVERING SELF-LOVE

It was during my Saturn Return that I first started to cultivate self-love and practise my own values. It was when I began questioning who I was as a person and what I wanted out of life, rather than just morphing myself into other people all the time and shapeshifting through life.

Self-love isn't a bubble bath with a glass of red wine. It involves deep work and true understanding of all the facets of your being. Self-love requires zero judgement. It requires kindness and patience, while taking complete responsibility for yourself. It's about acknowledging your triggers and working through them. And taking ownership over the part you play in every situation. There's power in being able to say 'Hey, I fucked up,' and in owning that. Self-love shouldn't be on the condition that we're going to get everything right all the time. It's being able to hold ourselves in accountable grace while allowing ourselves the room to learn from mistakes and grow.

Self-love has come through many Saturnian lessons for me. Through autonomy, authorising myself and discipline. As I have and will continue to say in this book, these were all foreign concepts to me for most of my life, but discipline is one of the greatest demonstrations of self-love. Being disciplined with our daily rituals over time increases both our mental and our physical well-being. Discipline when it comes to abstaining from toxic people, substances, trash TV or junk food. Discipline with cultivating our values and standing by them. Being disciplined with our boundaries. Discipline in respect of saying no. This sort of discipline is self-love. It communicates 'I am worthy of receiving, and this is what I don't tolerate.' For a recovering people-pleaser

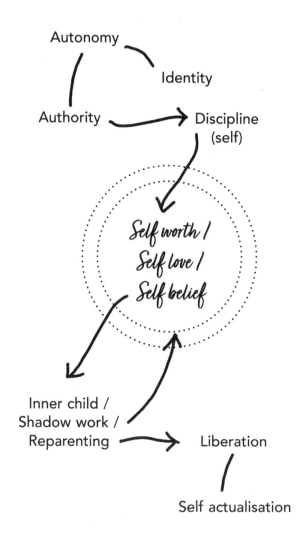

like me, who has an anxious attachment style, this has felt terrifying. But by trying to please everyone, you'll only end up disappointing yourself.

BOUNDARIES

Boundaries are easy enough to fathom. We can compute what they are and throw the word around, but building and communicating them is a whole different story. Like I've said before, unconditional love doesn't mean unconditional tolerance. Boundaries are actually a point of connection and a way to protect ourselves and our relationships. So, how do we know when we need to set one?

One of the ways we can tell when a boundary is needed is by listening to the signals our body is giving us when communicating with friends, family members, colleagues and partners.

Do we feel expanded? Or do we feel depleted? Is that person or situation making you feel small? Cornered? Anxious? Or safe? Listen to your body. When faced with a situation where we feel triggered, it can be helpful to practise the following exercise. I use this for tapping into my intuitive knowing, which allows me to get out of my head and know when I need to set a boundary. If you are struggling with a decision, unsure whether a boundary is being crossed – use the below as a compass to help you navigate any situation:

1. Take yourself to a calm and quiet place.

2. Tune into your breath.

3. Breathe deeply, in through your nose and out through your mouth.

4. Close your eyes and clear your mind.

5. Visualise the situation at hand and give your body two scenarios. In scenario one, you make the decision to say yes to the invitation or opportunity presented to you.

6. You may have an instant response or reaction. Your physicality may contract or expand, tense or soften. Once your body has responded, take note.

7. Scenario two: you decide to say no.

8. Notice the response or reaction. Whatever it is, there is usually a strong polarity between the two. Follow whichever one gives you a sense of calm.

9. You should have your answer about the situation and know what to do.

For me, one feels prickly, like harsh pins and needles, uncomfortable, constricted. The other is expansive, displaying shivers or tingles that feel good. You may experience it totally differently, but they will feel like opposites. This is not only how we can tap into our intuition, but also how to know when to set a boundary.

If you're like me, you'll be thinking, 'How can I set a boundary and still make everyone else happy?' I'm sorry to tell you that's not always possible.

A dear friend of mine gave me some amazing advice when it comes to making these decisions and setting boundaries. He said, 'You must have ruthless compassion.'

I've always struggled with not wanting to seem mean or disagreeable. Ruthless compassion is a great phrase because it allows us to remain in our heart space, to be compassionate to others but ruthless in our knowing and our conviction about what is right or wrong for us. It doesn't make us unkind, or bad people.

Upsetting others by setting a boundary can feel triggering. It may take you back to times when you learned and were conditioned to believe it wasn't safe to set a boundary or state your needs. If particular moments and events are coming up, it's a good time to get curious:

- Journal around it.

- How did you feel?

- Did you have an emotional response? If so, that's OK.

- Remind yourself that you're no longer that version of yourself, nor are you in that situation anymore.

- Tell yourself that you can support and hold space for your inner child.

- Notice what could have been done differently.

- When do you wish you could have spoken up but remained silent?

- Where did you compromise yourself and feel like your boundaries were being crossed?

- Now, whatever feels more comfortable for you, either as the version of you then or the version you are now, say what you wish you'd said, to whomever needed to hear it.

- Repeat it over and over if you wish.

- Sit with that for a moment.

- Now, how do you feel?

You probably feel expanded. Boundaries are about living in alignment with our integrity and it isn't based on a specific outcome. It's about what is your responsibility, where you end and another begins. One person's comfort might be another person's limits. But when communicated, we can bridge the gap between the two. It's in the act of speaking what we feel, living by our principles and trusting we can hold ourselves in that process. This is a constant practice, but so worthwhile. Because the more you exercise it, the more you realise that people will respect your boundaries if you uphold them. By being the example, you can invite them to do the same for themselves.

AUTONOMY

Autonomy is an interesting piece of the puzzle when it comes to navigating your Saturn Return, in addition to how it affects and influences your relationships, both personal and professional. By definition, autonomy is the capacity to make an informed, uncoerced decision. Autonomy is about a person's ability to act on his or her own values, virtues and interests. The word is taken from the Greek word *autonomos* which means 'self-governance' ('autos' meaning self 'monos' meaning law). It means we have a good sense of what matters to us individually. This can be challenged by oppressive social hierarchy and the systems that govern us, but during Saturn's Return, you'll notice a yearning for your own autonomy. Personal autonomy narrows down who and what we authentically align with, giving us a compass for the direction we are heading. Because when we stop bending to other people's expectations and needs, and start honouring our own principles and virtues, we create freedom. Freedom to be ourselves and freedom over our lives.

Collectively, self-autonomy allows for healthy debate. In many ways, we've lost the ability to sit with friends who hold different beliefs and ideas to ourselves. As if someone communicating a different point of view or perspective invalidates our own. In this 'cancel culture' society, there seems to be little room for nuance. A secure, autonomous person, however, isn't threatened by another person's point of view. They invite it. In order to refine ourselves we must be open to new ideas, new possibilities and then discern for ourselves what feels right, not go proclaiming our virtuousness to others. Once we cultivate these principles within ourselves and start living by them, this might require us to be the black sheep in our families or society. When everyone else is following a narrative that doesn't ring true for you, to stand unwaveringly by your values, you may become an outlier. Another bittersweet victory.

When a person lacks autonomy, they're more controlled by what others think, say, feel and do. They'll adapt and defer to other people's opinions. Autonomy stops our need for validation and our need to fit in, which will feel uncomfortable at first because as we practise it, it'll rub up the sides of other people who are used to our lack of boundaries and autonomy and have gained from them. It also allows us to step into a secure place within ourselves, with our values, virtues and beliefs, so that people can come and go, agree or disagree without our sense of self crumbling as they do. Our values and beliefs are unique to us and are our infrastructure for a life of harmony.

When it comes to relationships, if you've spent most of your life romanticising co-dependent love (which we often do), it's unbalanced and often intense, autonomous love feels unsafe at first because of the space that's in between. We often expect our romantic partners to hang up their autonomous boots and become beholden to us. And vice versa. Saturn has taught me that developing a sacred union, a conscious partnership, requires freedom. You have to accept the other person has their needs, wants and desires separate to you, just as you have yours. And you're not responsible for each other's happiness.

That isn't to say you won't support each other or be there for each other, or try to make each other happy, but you aren't responsible for it. There's a big difference. Nor are you responsible for each other's healing. Feeling the burdening sense of responsibility for another's happiness and healing eventually leads to resentment. Once autonomy starts slipping in a relationship, so does our sense of identity. This can lead to contempt. Equally, the more we cultivate autonomy in our life and relationships, the stronger our sense of identity gets. In turn, the more fruitful and meaningful our relationships become. We have to give ourselves and others permission to be our fullest expression of self and trust the space in between.

AUTHORITY

During our Saturn transits and oppositions, the theme of authority appears again and again. Each Saturn transit brings with it lessons in authority. From authority comes discipline, which we've established we need, but if we don't learn to authorise ourselves, to give ourselves the permission to be the authority over our own lives, we'll seek it from outside.

Towards the end of my turbulent and reckless twenties, I began to crave authority. Something I'd rejected and rebelled against for most of my life. I continued to seek it outside of myself, as it didn't occur to me that authority could be found within me.

Each Saturn square and opposition that occurs every seven years gives a nudge to this theme. Authority can be especially prevalent in the context of family dynamics. You only need to reflect on your behaviour towards your teachers and parents at ages fourteen and twenty-one to recognise the rebellious streak flare up, pushing against authority figures. But we don't have the maturity or self-awareness we need yet. During your Saturn Return, however, we can hopefully handle this shift with more grace.

Like our Saturn square at fourteen when we become physically more adult and go through puberty, our Saturn Return can also be an awkward phase in our coming of age. It's during this time when you notice a lot of people suddenly questioning how their parents parented them and where they might have fallen short. Perhaps you feel you had to take responsibility before you were appropriately capable, adopting a caretaker role too young, taking care of those who were supposed to be taking care of you. Or maybe, like me, you resisted taking responsibility altogether.

This can manifest in a co-dependent relationship between parent and child, both reinforcing and affirming each other's roles and not stepping into their new stages of life. As many will become parents themselves during this time, these things come up so we can choose whether to repeat the cycles or do things differently. Honouring our own voice and not just replicating the voices of those around us. An opportunity to create new rules rather than continue to live by somebody else's.

It's worth looking closely at your chart for how this might show up for you. This moment invites us to heal from the past, so we don't repeat the same mistakes on autopilot and in turn have history repeat itself. If we can lean into our heart space and have compassion for those who raised us, if we can recognise their limitations based on their upbringing, we can begin to heal generationally.

The wish for parental validation is hard to avoid. Why do you think Christmas is so triggering for people? Everyone knows that regardless of how you're treated at work, no matter how far up on the economic ladder you are, or what you've achieved in your life, when you go home for Christmas, you feel eleven years old again. You find yourself seeking your parents' approval across the kitchen table while carving the turkey, feeling like a failure because they've casually dismissed your recent accolade, more consumed by the roast potatoes.

As adults, we're often still driven by parental validation, even if our parents aren't around anymore. During our Saturn Return, however, and as we embark on a more spiritual path, we're invited to step up and become our own authority. The best way to handle this is to acknowledge the separation between whatever you experienced as a child and where you are now. To have the awareness of both the child within and the person you've become. Once you have awareness of these two dynamics, you can hopefully gain enough space from the emotional triggers to know when your inner child has been activated. You feel it and acknowledge it, but you don't need to react in the way you once did. You can self-soothe that inner child and hold space for it yourself. What does it need? Does it need to be held? Comforted? Loved? Can you provide this for yourself?

In the spiritual world, this practice is often called 'reparenting' or inner child work. This process doesn't mean cutting off from your parents. Nor does it mean you love them any less. You just don't need their approval like a child does. (Especially if it's a futile pursuit.)

The way we receive and internalise information doesn't mean that's how it was intended. Through the prism of someone else's lens lives a different story, based on its own conditions and limitations. Julia Samuels spoke to me about this when she came on the podcast for a second time. She told me that if we can 'look up' at the stories and lineage before us, we'll better understand the behaviours of those around us and have more compassion.

We have to dismantle the scaffolding of our own reality and make space for someone else's to find mutual ground. So, if you can, and your situation allows for it, use your Saturn Return as an opportunity to see what your relationships with your family members and other loved ones both did and do for you. Appreciate the sacrifices they made and forgive their shortcomings, and, where they did fall short, know that you can provide yourself with the security and safety you needed. You can liberate yourself from the story you've been telling yourself. A story that might be disempowering to you or a thought you've lived by that's weighing you down.

During this process of liberation that comes about during one's Saturn Return, what we're ultimately uncovering is that we are in fact our own authority now. And there's a necessary friction in this process. You're now capable of carving out your own reality. Whatever texture you wish it to be, whatever colour, pattern, shape or size, it's yours. You are the architect of your life, so why not make it extraordinary? By all means invite your parents in – and anyone else, for that matter. But if they start to criticise your choice in wallpaper, don't sweat it. You didn't create it for them. You created it for you. And remember, everyone is viewing the world through their own lens. There are infinite realities simultaneously existing. Your reality is your only responsibility.

I've witnessed a lot of people going through this transit and resisting this opportunity. In many ways, I did, too. But, this can cause one to remain in a childlike state. It creates a lack of assertiveness, an inability to stand our ground in our thoughts and opinions, and sometimes a struggle when it comes to finding a conscious and equal romantic partnership that we might be yearning for. It can also put in a stopper in terms of career progression.

The message you're sending to the Universe is 'I'm not ready for this initiation yet'. Though of course, there will always be another opportunity down the line to rise to the challenge. It isn't something you can get wrong; the Universe doesn't work like that. The lesson just comes back round again and again. The Universe will send you signs. It'll throw pebbles in your track, subtly trying to guide you. But if you keep ignoring it and resisting it, it might start throwing rocks or boulders. We can listen now or later. But in order to grow, we must listen.

My advice is to pay attention to the pebbles before the boulders roll in. (I wish I had!) Becoming the authority in your life and this process of shifting family dynamics isn't a straightforward one. Your aim (if possible) is to arrive at a harmonious place within your family in this new role. Pay attention to the energy you feel when communicating and when you're spoken to in a certain way. Perhaps you were the one who was always put down by others or blamed for things.

Remember, the process of establishing new boundaries to autonomy and authority in this new stage of life isn't an easy one. The first step is setting energetic boundaries in solitude. Don't go announcing it or proclaiming it just yet – you're not seeking a reaction or response. The first and most important step is establishing where you're at in *your-self*. Can you hold space for yourself? Can you separate the adult you've become from the child within? And where are you going to draw that energetic line? Then when a family member, or anyone talks to you in a way that feels disempowering or regressive, you'll know when to speak up.

When it comes to exercising your authority in family dynamics and relationships, it's not about proclaiming your new-found sense of self from a place of ego. It is all about understanding, kindness, boundaries and communication.

- Understanding: to have understanding of someone else's experience. To have empathy. To create the space for their perspective.

- Kindness: kindness is everything. And never mistake kindness for weakness. The strongest people I know are the kindest. Whatever you do, make it kind. Even when faced with hate and adversity, meet it with kindness – it always wins.

- Boundaries: boundaries are the foundations to your authority and personal sovereignty. They aren't the same as walls. And they need . . .

- Boundaries need to be communicated. We cannot expect someone to magically know how we feel, so we have to communicate, even when it feels uncomfortable to do so.

Within my own family, I grew up as the creative, dyslexic one in a family of academics. I often felt like an outlier. My mum would take me to get extra help outside school and it was clear then that I wasn't someone who thought in a linear way. She always very sweetly and proudly reminds me how highly I scored on the emotional intelligence test, but my struggles with spelling and algebra made me feel different – and schooling usually celebrates and values one type and measure of intelligence. I carried this belief that

I wasn't academic as a limitation throughout most of my life. I didn't want to ask questions because I didn't want to come across as stupid. I often struggled with simple tasks in silence. I didn't want to speak up in case I was left feeling embarrassed.

During my Saturn Return, I noticed how this carried through my other relationships and the way I went about things. In turn, as a result I kept getting stuck. If I didn't know the answer, I'd stop in my tracks and freeze rather than ask for help. When something happened that I wanted to question, I remained silent in case it caused an argument. Ironically, my career post-Saturn Return is based on asking questions. And I'm also constantly challenged to speak up and handle conflict in all other aspects. By no means have I mastered it. But it gets easier every time.

Ultimately, I had to reframe my view of myself. Of the things I felt ashamed about and assumed truths I had. Somehow, I had to turn those limitations into ladders in order to authorise myself. Once I realised my path or way of thinking wasn't linear, I embraced the squiggliness and the messiness of my mind. I saw the vastness of my emotions as a strength, not a weakness. Because they're what make me, me.

Have you ever felt like you were too much, too sensitive, too emotional, too loud or too anything? Subconsciously, we may gravitate towards people who will perpetuate this narrative and then we start to believe it ourselves. It's our unconscious bias. But let me tell you this: *you* aren't too anything. Don't collapse yourself trying to fit into the shapes and sizes of other people's expectations or needs. If you find yourself diminishing your light because it's too bright for someone's eyes, this is an opportunity to authorise yourself enough to walk away from anyone who tells you you're 'too' anything. Find liberation in owning your wholeness.

Saturn ultimately wants us to cultivate sovereignty over ourselves and authority over our lives, meaning we clash with external authority figures in this process as we reclaim it. Ask yourself: How is Saturn guiding me or challenging me to be my own authority?

My willingness to subcontract my own authority stemmed from a multitude of things, but ultimately, it was from fear that if I set a boundary, I'd be abandoned and rejected. I have, however, learned that if any relationship, friendship or career falls apart by me setting boundaries, it wasn't mine to keep.

SOBER CURIOUS

It's little surprise that in my Saturnian quest for authenticity and personal sovereignty, drinking was my greatest hurdle. It had become my vehicle to escape myself for so long – my means for shapeshifting. People worry that they're missing out by not drinking. But trust me – I missed out on a lot more by drinking!

There were nights I don't remember a thing, yet I'd be walking, talking and fully animated. I didn't have an off-switch. And I'd chase the night through to the morning sun, not caring about the repercussions. This was most present during my hedonistic early twenties, when I thought I was invincible. During my Saturn Return, I realised that I was only human. Fragile in ways I didn't expect, I've seen first-hand the grips of addiction. I could see the possibility of it down the track if I didn't change course.

So I started questioning my mindset around drinking. I started exploring my internal world, stepping into the dark and empty spaces I'd always filled with substances. I don't regret anything, and I've garnered enough stories and anec-dotes to last a lifetime. I'd never take back those years, but my decision to adopt a more sober lifestyle was the best one I ever made.

My relationship with alcohol and having to come to terms with the fact that me and alcohol weren't a good combination felt like a very inconvenient truth. One that took years to admit. I experimented with this throughout my twenties by altering the variables, each time hoping for different results. Just drinking on the weekends, the three-drinks-only rule, just drinking wine. Just drinking tequila, or my personal favourite: champagne. You name it, I tried it.

But when the results came in, the graph of my life and mental health would take a dramatic downwards spike whenever alcohol came into the mix. It was undeniable.

Alcohol had been my potion for shapeshifting, my method and means to be whoever I needed to be to fit in. A belief I'd lived with for so long that gave me a false sense of belonging. So, who would I be without it? Oh! that's right. I'd have to be me. Whoever that was.

My commitment to becoming my true self solidified during my Saturn Return and I knew that lifting the mask meant leaning into sobriety. Abstaining from alcohol also meant abstaining from my need to morph into someone else. One of the hardest things about sticking to it was the lack of community. It was so ingrained in me (especially as a Brit) that drinking was what you do. Whether in mourning, in victory or loss. You raise a glass for sorrow and celebration just the same. As far as I knew at the time, there was AA and then there was everybody else. It seemed I wasn't able to do 'normal drinking', but I wasn't in need of AA, either. So where did I fit? Turns out there's a whole spectrum on which to land.

It was when I discovered *Sober Curious* – a podcast and term coined by Ruby Warrington – that I felt like I'd found a space and language that resonated with me. Sober curious means you have the option to choose – to question or change your drinking habits for health-focused reasons. It's less binary and means I don't get friends giving me strange looks if I use red wine in a cooking dish or if I try someone else's wine, wondering if a whiff is going to make me fall off the wagon. Sober curious means I can drink if I want, but 99 per cent of the time I don't. I grant myself the freedom to have a drink on a rare occasion, but I also know and am aware of the risks and repercussions. This might be something I outgrow, as it's the remnant of not entirely being able to let go of that part of my identity. Some think I'll reprogramme my whole relationship with alcohol. In all honesty, at this point I'm not entirely sure.

For a long time I felt insecure when not drinking in social settings. I still occasionally battle with this. But strangely, sometimes I feel more confident when I'm sober, because alcohol only momentarily masks our insecurities and charges us interest in the morning.

My first bit of advice on this very complex subject is that everyone's relationship with alcohol is unique and personal and should be treated as such. I've had to handle my fair share of 'Why don't you drink?' and 'Why are you being boring?' And yes, it's a pain. I tend to go with the less-is-more approach now. I don't need to tell my life story to a stranger at a bar or at a dinner party. A simple 'I don't really drink' will suffice. Frankly, it's no one's business and people have to earn that story from me.

Alcohol is just a normalised, socially accepted drug – and can be a very harmful one at that. So, if you're waking up to the fact it doesn't work for you, well done. And I salute you on this journey! I know it isn't an easy one. When you stop or cut down, I'd also advise that you go to as many social things as you can during this time. It's easy to stay sober at home watching Netflix in your PJs, but go to where you'll be most triggered and feel the need to drink . . . By giving yourself a new experience in those settings and abstaining, you'll find it far easier to manage and you'll discover new tools for how to handle those situations in the future.

Check in with yourself when your need to drink feels activated. Take yourself off for a moment and try to think about tomorrow's you, instead of the need to alleviate whatever discomfort you're feeling. Long-term pleasure, short-term pain. Short-term pleasure, long-term pain. Which would you rather choose?

After a couple of victories waking up feeling like a million dollars rather than like you've just poisoned yourself, you'll start to find it a whole lot easier. And believe me when I say sober isn't boring. Sober is sexy, it's clear skin, white eyes, a clear head. A happy mind. I laugh just as much and I have just as much fun. The big difference is the connections are authentic. I'm not befriending some random person I came across in the loo at a party. In fact, perhaps I have fewer friends. But they're real friends for the right reasons. Who would never make me feel like I need to be anything else, other than who I am.

At twenty-nine, I remember driving to a friend's birthday party in the countryside. I knew few people there, so I was nervous, shy at the thought of going alone. At this point I'd tried many periods of sobriety, but it hadn't quite stuck – and big parties were always where I faltered. So I avoided them altogether. It was a three-hour drive and I listened to Ruby Warrington's *Sober Curious* podcast the whole way there. As everyone started to get a little loose at the party and people scuttled off two by two to the bathroom to powder their nose, I remember thinking that perhaps this was my time to leave. This was the elusive 'French exit' I'd heard so much about but never experienced.

As I drove back to the Airbnb I was staying in alone, I did feel a little lonely. I was used to being the last woman standing, so being the first to leave was foreign to me. When I got back, I realised I'd actually had an amazing time. I was also far more engaged with who I was sitting next to at dinner, rather than focusing on where my next drink was coming from. When I woke, I didn't have that swell of regret and anxiety washing over me. I felt a sense of pride and I often think of this as one of the first times I'd practised self-love. I'd chosen myself over the need to fit in. And it felt amazing. I continued to create these experiences, these little wins, and as I did, my confidence grew.

UNLEARNING LIMITING BELIEFS

Often, the biggest obstacles to growth are our beliefs: assumed truths, picked up throughout our lives by osmosis. Our inability to handle conflict, our perfectionism, our negative view of self and our low self-worth all come down to our limiting beliefs. This may manifest in bad finances, sabotaging relationships, in our career and or in personal life. In our Saturn Return, we're forced to reckon with some of these limiting beliefs and start to unpick them.

The first step in addressing your limiting beliefs is identifying them. Noticing your patterns. Once you identify them, see what they've resulted in. Once you notice that negative cycle, you'll realise that although these belief systems are a product of the mind trying to keep you safe, they're counterintuitive to your own growth and development. We can then create a new narrative, and a new behaviour and a new pattern.

Identifying the origin of the beliefs is also important. Consider the following:

- Where did each belief stem from?

- Next, think of times when those thoughts were in fact inaccurate.

- Then replace the limiting self-belief with a new one that aligns and better supports you.

The trickiest part is recognising it, as it becomes so entrenched as an internalised truth and belief that we don't even realise it's happening. Our neural pathways want to repeat the familiar root they've always taken – even if it's the more painful path.

Repeating the same patterns and mistakes again and again can be the source of much unnecessary anxiety that isn't based in any sort of reality. For example, as I've mentioned many times already in this book, I've always found it incredibly hard to deal with conflict. At such times, I usually adopt a head-in-the-sand approach, hoping that when I resurface things will have miraculously resolved themselves. As I mentioned before, Saturn rests in my third house, which represents communication. So it's always been my challenge and karma to learn how to communicate the word 'no' and create healthy boundaries. If you're a recovering people-pleaser like me, you'll know this is agonisingly uncomfortable.

I've also long held the belief 'I am terrible with money.' But as one of my dear friends and mindset coach Africa Brooke reminded me, 'Is that *actually* true?' Instead, she encouraged me to replace the statement with 'I am getting much better with my finances and money.'

Doing the 'work' in tracing back where these might have stemmed from is fascinating. It might be from sibling or family dynamics, or early school experiences. But undoing societal, parental or family conditioning takes a lot of hard work. Things will come up that are difficult to look at. Shame may arise. But we have to feel it to heal it.

Whatever thoughts or feelings you have about yourself that you have internalised as an identity piece that are disempowering, try these next tools for reprogramming your mind and letting them go. It can be scary, as we don't like change and we fear the alternative outcome. But by practising and reinforcing new and affirming beliefs, we begin to make permanent positive changes to our behaviour and our lives. Feel free to take notes as we go through these steps together:

Step One: Identify your limiting beliefs.
Be specific in terms of what area you're covering. This could be love, relationships, trust, money and finance. Even lifestyle, organisational skills, your body and health. Anything!

Step Two: Name the emotion.
What emotion comes up for you when you write this down? Name it. It might be sadness, shame, guilt, fear, etc. Take the time to write it down.

Step Three: Get curious ... Name the source.
Acknowledge where these beliefs might have come from. Is it parents? Childhood? School? Peers?

Step Four: Forgiveness.
Forgive the source. Forgive whomever this belief stemmed from. Fully leaning into your heart space. Then, forgive yourself. Chastising yourself for being one way or

another keeps you in a cycle of shame, where you become stuck, repeating the same pattern. In order to move past these beliefs, we have to forgive ourselves for having them and forgive anyone who may have caused them.

Step Five: Say thank you to the beliefs and the emotion.

This may sound counterproductive, but it's important to acknowledge that those beliefs and the emotion that guards them served you at one point. They were a reaction to something in your life to keep you safe, and although not helpful anymore, they may have served a purpose at some point. We heal our emotions when we acknowledge them.

Now, replace these beliefs with a positive, more affirming narrative that aligns with you today – but make it realistic. Don't go from 'I am terrible with money' to 'I am incredible with money.' Start with 'I am becoming much better at handling my finances.' Remember: baby steps! You can repeat this process in a couple of months and up the ante!

By honouring this process, we accept the necessity of what we've experienced. But that doesn't mean we have to carry it with us. Journalling is such a powerful tool for working with subconscious beliefs. Try free flow writing, which is writing without thinking about what you're saying in a stream of consciousness. The 'Morning Pages' ritual by Julia Cameron from her book *The Artist's Way* is a daily practice where you write three pages in the morning before doing anything else. It's not thought about, it's not a diary entry – it's whatever comes up for you, a distillation of thoughts from the subconscious mind so you can get out of your own way and begin your day. Try it out, you'll be surprised by what comes up . . .

**Use this space to make notes around
your limiting beliefs:**

_____

_____

_____

_____

_____

_____

_____

_____

_____

_____

_____

_____

_____

_____

_____

_____

QUARTER-LIFE CRISIS

Shortly after returning to London, I started speaking with a schoolfriend from when I was much younger. Steph was the year above me and I hadn't seen her in about eleven years. We'd recently reconnected on social media and I could see she'd gone down a spiritual path, now running a retreat in Malaga called the 'Quarter Life Project' (now called Medicine Space). She invited me to go on one of the retreats, but I felt a lot of resistance and had reservations. I was in such a funk at that point that I wasn't sure whether it would push me over the edge.

In the end, I decided to go. It was just before my twenty-ninth birthday. On my arrival in Malaga, I immediately felt unsure. We were a group of women all around the age of thirty who were there because they were struggling in some way. My ego kicked in big time and I just wanted to get the hell out. I was planning my escape route on my phone, when Steph approached me.

'You're resisting,' she said.

Damn straight, I thought. I don't belong here!

'This just isn't for me,' I sheepishly rescinded, slightly scared of Steph, as she'd always been the 'cool girl'.

She nodded and said, 'Just give it the day.'

Which I couldn't really argue with. So I closed the Easy-Jet flight app on my phone and committed to the day.

We were taken to a hall, where we each spread out across it. Music started playing and we were instructed to dance. One of my worst nightmares was being realised. It was called 'free movement' or 'intuitive dance'. I'd never done it before and felt so uncomfortable. I'd usually only ever approach the dance floor after several vodkas! Stone-cold sober in broad daylight with a group of complete strangers was my idea of hell.

As tempted as I was to rush back to my phone and get the EasyJet app up on my screen again, I started to move to the music. After a while, I dropped out of my head and into my body – and in that moment, something changed. It's hard to say what exactly it was, but I'd been so disconnected from my body for so long, it was like therapy for the relationship between mind and body. They were finally talking. All the emotion that was stored in my body started to surface. The tears started to come. As I moved and cried, something in me changed. I didn't leave that day. I went on to have one of the most transformative weeks of my life.

Before this point, I felt like the Universe was conspiring against me. I was in such a victimhood mentality, unable to see the role I played in anything. But once I unlocked that puzzle piece that perhaps things weren't happening to me, but for me, things slowly began to shift. I stepped to the side of the roadblock in my mind that I'd viewed as a dead end and I kept walking.

Now, a tricky part of shifting your mentality and your

relationship with responsibility is that all the blame you've been projecting elsewhere suddenly feels like it has no direction but to fall onto you. Blaming yourself isn't the same as taking responsibility. It's actually another way of playing the victim. But there are two things you must maintain when doing this kind of work. 1) curiosity, and 2) zero judgement.

If your best friend suddenly told you they realised they hadn't taken responsibility for their life so far, you wouldn't beat them up about it. You'd support them in their realisation. Nothing can grow from shame. The reason we struggle to progress in life is because of our inability to acknowledge where we need to do the work or where we might have failed – because we identify with that part too much. We'd rather stay in our limiting, familiar stories than pierce the bubble with a different truth, even if that leads to a better outcome.

During your Saturn Return, you'll be faced with the manifestations of the last three decades – every decision you've made up until now. No wonder it's regarded as the midlife crisis for 'almost thirty'. But I believe that a huge part of this discomfort is because of the shame we experience and the isolation we create as a result.

Although unique to you and your experience, the reality is that everyone is facing their own Saturnian challenges and everyone experiences shame. When shame is added into the mix, it's much, much harder to navigate your way through.

For the last few years of my twenties, I felt ashamed of myself. I felt I didn't amount to what I'd hoped. I was often at war with my body and I could be my own worst enemy. My Saturn Return forced me to confront everything and come to terms with the reality of where I was at in life.

HEALING OUR RELATIONSHIP WITH OUR BODIES

Noura's astrological insight:

In the chakra system, Saturn is associated primarily with the root chakra. The root chakra, also called the Mūlad-hara chakra, is associated with the roots of what makes us feel safe, nourished, healthy and steady. It gives us a feel-ing of worthiness. It's self-regulating of our desires and it's grounding but also that which is wild, physical, feminine, sexual. That which makes us feel safe in the expression of our sexuality and that which fuels creativity. Whenever we find an imbalance in any of the aforementioned, be it an excess in it or a compulsive repression, it means there's an imbalance in the root chakra which, in turn, can cause an imbalance in how Saturn expresses itself throughout our lives.

We need to feel safe to feel sexual and sensual. We need to feel nourished and to have our basic needs met to find space to explore our femininity and our physical bodies. We need a consistent, steady routine to be able to fuel our wild side which, in turn, inspires both us and those around us. All of this is where we need to begin in order to heal ourselves and our relationship with our bodies. It's where we can learn to love every beautiful way our bodies express themselves. Using the mantra 'LAM' or listening to it cleanses and heals the root chakra during a meditative or creative practice. Not only can this slowly help to heal this chakra, but it also triggers us energetically, so that we start a relationship with our bodies where we feel both contained and free.

I'd say my mind–body relationship began to lose its harmony all the way back when I was seventeen or eighteen. While I was growing up, I was always very small and slight. In fact, I was always the smallest in my class. Which I hated, of course, because we always want what we don't have. How I longed to be tall and curvy . . . Or at least, have any kind of curve at all.

When my parents got divorced, I was fifteen. In terms of development, I was still very behind all the other girls at school, who wore bras and had started their periods. Boys were looking at them differently and I was like their small sidekick who didn't get a look-in. I believed that if I ate enough, I'd grow taller, curvy and get big boobs. Sadly, it doesn't work like that. I started eating an enormous amount in the hope that said breasts would arrive (they didn't).

As I've just mentioned, sadly, this didn't encourage boobs, curves or a growth spurt. Instead, I started putting on weight in all the wrong places. By this point, I'd started to equate a feeling of fullness with one of love and safety. Perhaps because during this time, my life was disrupted. As anyone whose parents have got divorced will know, it can be very unsettling. Even though divorce is incredibly common, it can still have a traumatic impact.

When I arrived at boarding school, I suddenly wasn't so sure about this calorie-rich diet I'd been on. Girls there were competitively dieting and during this time, there was little education around nutrition. It was less 'nourish yourself' and more here's a nibble of cheese so you don't faint. So I followed the trend and I stopped eating. In a short space of time, I lost a huge amount of weight. I was skipping meals, eating very 'healthily' when I did eat, and I was exercising every night after school. Sometimes twice a day, followed by chain-smoking on the school grounds and drinking Diet Coke to curb my hunger.

This started to give me the feeling of being in control, which made me feel safe. I quickly started looking way too thin and my strange behaviour around food became noticeable. My family was worried. I remember going wakeboarding with my brother that summer and I couldn't get up. My arms were like little spaghetti strings dragging me through the water, barely able to hold on.

The real turning point was seeing my first love again – the one I met when I was fifteen. We rekindled our romance (for the third year in a row) that summer, but when he came to stay with me in the Isle of Wight, he sat me down and said I needed to put on weight and start eating more. I sensed that this was an ultimatum and was so terrified of losing him that within about ten seconds, I was scoffing down a bowl of cheesy pasta.

Weight wise, I 'normalised'. Mentally, it didn't go. This disconnection continued throughout my twenties. It was a feast or famine. Devour or deprivation. I was so out of touch with my body that I was rarely thinking about nourishing it. Instead, I was always thinking about its worth and that worth was dependent on it being a certain size. When I deprived myself, I felt in control. When I ate, I felt love. It's strange when you recognise that the very same voice that tells you 'you're too fat' also tells you to eat the entire cake. That voice isn't your friend, and it isn't you.

My weight would fluctuate, which would perpetuate this toxic cycle of shame. In turn, I then wouldn't want to go out or see anyone, convinced I looked so hideous that the outside world mustn't see me. There was a version of myself I was longing to be that always felt out of reach. This was one of the main reasons I went to therapy, shortly after my thirtieth birthday. And if this is something that resonates with you, I really do suggest seeking professional help from a therapist if you possibly can. It's a worthwhile investment to reframe this very corrosive narrative and write a different story.

I'd become so accustomed to this voice living in my head that I thought it would be there forever. I thought it would dominate and dictate my life. During my Saturn Return, it was one of the things that intensified, but simultaneously, I felt I had the opportunity to change it. It occurred to me that maybe I didn't need to carry this feeling with me for life.

Now, as I write this today, I'm by no means immune to that internal critic. Or the societal pressures to be a certain weight or appease the unattainable standards of beauty. I'd be lying if I still said it doesn't affect me. But I would say I'm much closer to where I want to be in terms of my relationship with my body – though it is, of course, a constant journey and a work in progress.

CHECK IN WITH YOUR EMOTIONAL STATE

When people talk about self-love, it often feels very surface-level. Social media posts with bubble baths and candles. But what does self-love really mean and what does it look like?

We all have the capacity to speak horribly to ourselves, in a way we never would to a friend. On our journey to self-love, I believe that it isn't always effective simply to plaster on a positive affirmation, especially when our inner critic is saying the opposite. Our inner critic is guarding those limiting beliefs, that we listed out in the previous section. For example, when my inner critic says, 'You need to lose weight' or 'You're looking ugly,' the real core belief behind that is, 'I'm not worthy of unconditional love and belonging.' Ouch, right?

First, we must unearth our core beliefs, inspect them and ask, 'Where did this come from?' This can be painful, but it can also be cathartic. Try writing out what you say to yourself. Dispel it onto the page now and really observe the narrative, however hard that might be. Perhaps share it with someone with whom you feel safe. Remember: you need to bring it to your full awareness to heal it and make space for something new.

Contained in the prison of our minds, we can deny it to ourselves, but it'll spill out in illness, anxiety or depression. Our body will eventually let us know if we don't. We can't always paint it over with positivity – sometimes healing is messy. Once acknowledged, we might feel like shit for a few days as all that sadness comes to the surface. Think about all those unkind words we said to ourselves being released. Take time to sit with these feelings, acknowledging them in their fullness, and let them go.

A beautiful method in the next step of this healing process is the Ho'oponopono – a powerful Hawaiian prayer created by therapist Dr Ihaleakala Hew Len. In true Saturnian form, its principles are rooted in taking 100 per cent responsibility. It's about detangling ourselves from past hurt or trauma and erasing old memories and data that's keeping us trapped. The steps are: repentance, forgiveness, gratitude and love. Each time, the negative voice comes back, eventually swallowing you up and consuming you. Notice it. Acknowledge its presence. Locate where in your body you feel it most, be it the chest, throat or stomach. Place your hands on that part of you and repeat: 'I'm sorry. Forgive me. I thank you. I love you.'

The origin of the problem lies deep within the self. Which means only *you* can heal it. Another similar practice that I highly recommend is where I run my hands across my entire body, usually when in bed before going to sleep, and say 'I love you' to every part of it. Like I'm coating myself in love where those unkind words had lived before.

Over time, the love began to seep into every part of my body. I began looking at myself differently. I stopped obsessing over my weight and started enjoying my body. Moving it, caring for it, and doing things that made it feel alive and nourished. Like it was my most valuable instrument rather than an ornament. I started practising intuitive eating. I stopped avoiding food that I'd deemed 'bad'. Instead of this constant thought of must go on a diet and lose weight – which would inevitably cause me to eat more – I'd say to myself 'Eat whatever feels good to me right now.'

It's extraordinary how much our bodies change when we make peace with them. For the first time in years, my weight has been consistent, my body more balanced. It's not perfect, but that isn't the goal. I get moments where I feel I'm going back to old patterns, but I have the tools now for when I do.

This is an ongoing journey, and by no means an easy one. Recently, while recovering from an illness, my whole routine went out of the window. I was eating a lot of beige food as I had no taste, I couldn't leave the house and I noticed I'd put on a little weight. As I did, I noticed the dial of that voice increase a couple of notches again – the beratement was back . . .

I decided to speak to my friend about it, which was hard as I felt vulnerable. Once I spoke the words out loud, they definitely lost some of their power. I realised that this old thought had been there to keep me in check, but it was no longer necessary. I said the Ho'oponopono prayer. Then I looked at myself in the mirror and praised my body with love, with gratitude. Not for its physical attributes by society's standards, but for its ability to walk, breathe, move, keep me warm. Feel. I woke the next day and saw myself totally differently.

Write down what you wish for your body. It might be: 'I have a balanced, harmonious relationship when it comes to eating and food.' It might not feel true right away, but give it time and see what changes.

Use this space to list what you want for your body:

_____

_____

_____

_____

_____

_____

_____

_____

_____

_____

_____

_____

_____

_____

_____

_____

I'll start with some of my own:

- 'I can eat what I want and I give my body what it needs to thrive.'

- 'I move my body from a place of love, kindness and respect.'

- 'I honour my body and all its wisdom.'

Most importantly, give yourself kindness when you feel you deserve it least. Practise the Ho'oponopono prayer and see what changes for you.

WISDOM IN THE DARKNESS

I never wanted to acknowledge my struggles with my mental health.

Mental health, like physical health, needs constant maintenance and care. It might not always be working efficiently or effectively. Everyone looks at things differently and mental health is stigmatised because it can't be seen and, quite frankly, because it scares people. People liken it to a broken leg, but it's not like that. It's not a 'bandage it up and fix it' kind of thing.

I was about twelve years old when I was first aware that something felt slightly different. I had these periods of melancholy, feeling insular and isolated. I was a happy kid in general – on the outside, to people around me and probably my family, too – but this other, melancholic aspect of myself I intuitively kept hidden. I began writing poetry when I felt this way as a source of escapism and to transmute my feelings into something else, dispelling them from my head. Because as sad as some of them were, the process of putting it down on paper and making it into something balanced and beautiful when it had felt ugly and twisted was always my medicine. It made it a kind of beautiful sadness, rather than a hopeless one, and somehow alchemised the pain. As I got older, however, I continued to hide away when these clouds came. No one ever really knew the depths of darkness I went to.

To describe my depression at its early stages now is odd. It feels like a giant thumb comes from the sky and just starts pushing down on me, putting pressure on my chest, pinning me to the floor. Or a dark cloud that arrives and looms over me. One that makes me question whether or not I'll ever see the sun again. It's not painful at first – it's just heavy. Breathing is heavy, living feels heavy. It can keep me motionless for a few days. And some periods are worse than others.

The one I've just come out of while writing this chapter was a bad one. At first, it felt like my head was just above water. Like my eyes were above the ocean and I could still see. Then suddenly I was immersed under. Not drowning, but not floating, either. Once that happens, I just have to ride it out. And the latest lasted two or three days. I try not to isolate myself completely, but it's hard, because I think there's often a lot of shame attached to feeling this way. My instinct is still to hide from the world. I cry a lot. It aches. It's like my heart is breaking and I have no idea why.

Then eventually, it slowly lifts, and moves along. There's little rhyme or reason for its arrival, or for when it chooses to go, but I am trying to figure out what triggers it (if anything). Perhaps a state of overwhelm. Too much internalised pressure and I combust. The inner critic in my head probably has a lot to answer for too, and is more closely tied into this than I'm aware. This is something I have by no means mastered, but by using the practices I wrote about above, I've noticed a huge difference. I don't think we acknowledge the effect our thoughts have on our bodies, the good and the bad.

Regardless of what brings it on, it's something I have to endure now and again – for the moment, anyway. I've become accustomed to treating it like an uninvited house guest who unexpectedly shows up once in a while. I've learned that it's better to invite it in than try to wrestle with it. To make it a cup of tea and take it upstairs to its bedroom, but not question how long it wishes to stay. Sometimes it says nothing, but other times it has something important to say. In the past I'd drink, escaping myself only to come back more plagued by its intensified presence.

When I feel this way, I find it hard to be around people, because I don't feel myself. At least, I don't feel the self I want to be.

Mental health is a spectrum, but what I will say is that through bad lifestyle choices and substance abuse, you can swiftly move along the scale to its darker corners. I've seen friends and family members do just this. And we might be predisposed to certain things, illnesses or conditions, but to a degree, there's also personal sovereignty at play when it comes to the mind and mental health.

Naturally, I didn't want to do irreparable damage to myself or my mind. But at twenty-three, I knew it was possible. I knew its fragility. I knew what it needed and what it didn't. And I'll admit, throughout the next five years I didn't always give it what it needed, often giving it what it didn't instead. I still hadn't quite accepted my responsibility in that.

How your loved ones react can also be challenging. It's difficult to see someone you love crying motionlessly for no apparent reason. To see their heart is breaking and you can't do anything about it is hard. I pride myself on being an effervescent and effusive person most of the time, but it's not sustainable 24/7. Sometimes, you just have to come undone.

In my thirty odd years, I've realised two things. One: life is seasonal. My depression is my winter, but it doesn't mean

I won't see summer again. And soon enough, I'll feel the sunlight. I'll see the autumn leaves and I'll move with it – and in doing so, enrich the texture and palette of my life and of my experience. Secondly, I may know the dark – I may have sat in it – but all things run even and I feel the light just as greatly.

If you're reading this and either experience something similar or know someone who does, remember that having someone there is really powerful. Not to talk it through necessarily, or to try to fix it, but just the presence of another human being, to know you are not alone. When someone allows me to witness this and lets me in, I know what a privilege that is – someone sharing their vulnerability is the ultimate gesture of trust. If you're unsure how to handle it or what to say in these situations, I recommend saying this: '*All* of you is welcome.' This encourages the other person to reclaim the exiled parts of themselves. To know it's OK to feel what they're feeling and that there's no shame in it.

Dear Self – a Poem

I wrote this to myself in my journal and wanted to share it for anyone reading this book who's going through something similar. I hope it might help. Often when I'm feeling this way, I write. Either poetry or just a distillation of thoughts. This has always been a tool for me, so perhaps it might encourage you to do the same and try writing a letter to yourself:

Dear Self.
Just like the weather, storms come and go.
But after they do, flowers soon grow.
I know it's hard to find the light, when you're alone in the dark.
But you haven't lost the fight or dimmed the spark.
It's just the quiet place where you sometimes go.
For how long, or how often, we never quite know.
But know this.
No matter how hard, these feelings won't last.
Remind yourself: this, too, shall pass.
You don't need to fix it; you don't have to pretend.
So, phone your mother, your brother or friend.
People want to be there to help in the end.
So if you're feeling alone,
Like the darkness has won,
Lean into it, let go, let yourself come undone.
Don't be ashamed – you're no less at all.
Just like autumn leaves, let yourself fall.
Cry if you must, for just like the rain,
This storm will soon pass,
And you'll blossom again.

If you feel called to, take the time now to write a 'Dear Self' poem or a letter to yourself to treasure going forwards:

_____

_____

_____

_____

_____

_____

_____

_____

_____

_____

_____

_____

_____

_____

_____

_____

_____

COMING HOME TO MYSELF

Noura's astrological insight:

The great work, our life's work and the slow uncovering process of it is a lot of what Saturn is about. But what about identity? When we're choosing a path – a path that feels close to our heart, that feels calm and productive yet never fatally discouraging, even when the obstacles test our tenacity – we're also discovering another layer of our identity.

It would be naive to assume that we've figured out our whole lives by the age of thirty, but it certainly wouldn't be an untruth to say we're closer to aligning with our soul's expression than we were before Saturn Returned. Often, when we're close to it, we start to question it. Generally, this is because we intuitively feel the commitment it'll require and we're not always as ready to embrace this, no matter how evolved we think we've become, so we tip-toe around it.

However, astrologically, identity relates a lot to the sun and the sun relates a lot to the truth. It's obvious – it was there all along. It was the clouds of insecurity, doubts, past traumas, naysayers and nebulous fantasies that prevented us from seeing the outline of who we truly are. What it is we stand for and how we want to be remembered, long after the sun has set. This is the gift that Saturn's Return leaves us with after all the turmoil and work we've done. This clear inner knowing of who we've been all along, if only we'd had the courage to see it for ourselves.

One of my intentions in writing this book was to create the handbook of life I wish I'd had during my Saturn Return. To understand that these experiences were not happening to me, they were happening for me. Writing this book has been a very cathartic and confronting process. It's been about excavating, layer upon layer all the things I thought I needed to be in this world and reconciling with the parts of me I hid away. I hope that it can do the same for you and has brought a little calm and solace into the chaotic messiness of life.

At times I have been scared to share my truth, in fear of being judged or being too much. A voice has whispered in my ear at many moments of writing: 'Everyone is going to think you are completely mad.' I have wrestled with my own self-doubt and criticism. I am telling you this to remind you that at no point do we suddenly become completely fixed, or immune from these very human feelings and thoughts, no matter where we get to. All we can hope is that we can better manage them to use them to our advantage, not to our detriment. To try our best and put truthful things out into the world regardless of the outcome. The world needs more truth. And a small act of courageous truth from you might not seem like it would be revolutionary, but remember, every drop contributes to the wave.

In my moments of hazy doubt, I will often get a message from someone who has been listening to the podcast, sharing how it has resonated with them and their experience. I received one recently that ended with, 'Thank you Caggie, I know we don't know each other but you feel like a close friend I have never met.' And the loveliest thing about that is, it goes both ways. I hope this book has evoked the same feeling for you. Although we might not know each other yet, I consider us friends from afar.

I also hope this book has reframed your view on Saturn. Although other common names for the planet (as mentioned at the start of this book) are the Grim Reaper and the Great Malefic, which doesn't really instil excitement when anticipating its arrival. The grim reaper personifies death, whilst the great malefic brings bad luck and misfortune. But in order to be reborn, there needs to be a death of sorts. Death of ego perhaps. Death of who you thought you needed to be. Not all deaths are bad. and after the 'bad luck', misfortunes and karmic lessons comes good fortune and a greater awareness of self. We cannot bypass one without the other, as I have said before, all things in life run even. So do not be afraid of what Saturn's Return might bring, be excited by the version of yourself you will blossom into on the other side.

Through this understanding and reflection, I can see now that maybe it is not Saturn we are afraid of, maybe we are just afraid of ourselves. We are afraid of who we would be if nothing was holding us back. If we unshackled ourselves from falsities, if we shed the illusion that external authorities and beliefs govern us, that everything would crumble. But if Saturn has taught us anything, it's that sometimes we need a reckoning.

Saturn will make you question everything and it will make you feel everything in a way you perhaps never have before. But it's worth it, all the messy, painful experiences are worth it because they are the path where you will learn compassion, empathy and strength. Just like the hand that sculpts the clay, this is the process of your becoming.

I believe our Saturn Return can be our moment to fall back in love with our lives and ourselves. It challenges us and, conversely, rewards us. As we mature with Saturn and hopefully come out the other side a more authentic, truthful version of ourselves, we can look back and realise perhaps Saturn wasn't such a punitive taskmaster, after all. Viewing Saturn from Earth, it's a spectacular and unique planet. And if you look at it from a different angle, its rings actually look like a halo (just like on the cover of this book). Reflecting the true nature of this planet, as a source of spiritual strength and guidance – for us all.

**And if Saturn has taught me anything,
it's that slowly is the fastest way to get to
where you need to be.**

I hope by reading this you understand that what Saturn ultimately seeks during your Saturn Return is your truth, your authenticity and the drawing out of your true potential. It may feel aggressive, ruthless even, in its methods, but thank God for Saturn. I'll continue my love affair with this great planet, because I know I still have more lessons to learn.

Remember: the journey is endless. How could it not be? After all, we're floating on a speck of dust through an infinite space, navigating both the cosmos around us and our internal world within. Listen closely for the dialogue between your inner and outer worlds, because when you hear it, you'll have a feeling of oneness with the Universe. And everything will make sense, if only for a fleeting moment.

I wish you luck on your quest for authenticity. I hope this book has given you a new insight and understanding. If you're feeling lost, look out for the spirit guides along the way. It would be an honour that by reading this, I might have been one for you.

Acknowledgements

To the team at Orion for trusting me to write this book and believing in me.

To Mylène, who designed this beautiful cover.

To my friends, my chosen family whom I love dearly.

To the community of Saturn Returns, my friends from afar.

To all the guests who have generously given their time to come on the *Saturn Returns* podcast and share their advice and experiences.

To my family: Mum, Dad, Ian, Alexandra and my brother Freddie.

To my partner Tom for your support and being my safest space. Thank you for teaching me what true love is.

To Noura, thank you for helping me bring this book to life. Your wisdom and friendship has been a constant guiding light.

To Sydney, my right-hand woman for keeping me together during the whole process. without whom this wouldn't have been possible!

Discover more at www.SaturnReturns.co.uk

and download

Saturn Returns with Caggie

wherever you get your podcasts.